ESCAPE FROM CENTRAL ASIA

ESCAPE FROM CENTRAL ASIA

By The Sirdar Ikbal Ali Shah

The Octagon Press

London

ISBN No: 90086078 2

Printed in England by Tonbridge Printers Ltd., Tonbridge Kent

CONTENTS

THE GOLDEN CARAVAN

The little wind which heralds the sun's rising stirred among the sands. A loud call resounded through the caravansarai, the cry of the muezzin calling to men to awake so that they might engage in morning prayer.

"*La Illaha Illallah* (There is no God but God)," he repeated. "Worship is better than sleep!" he continued in his holy chant.

In the red rays of the first hour of day our devotions were hastily offered, for we had far to go before the Imam gave the signal for journey's end that day.

As a perhaps over-devout fellow-pilgrim of mine from Konia said, the uproar of the caravan getting under way is like that of Eblis, the Devil, flapping his wings. The peculiar ululation of the camels, the incessant yelping of dogs, the cries of the camel-drivers and water-sellers, urging travellers to see that they are well supplied with liquid refreshment, and the noisy farewells of friends combine to make a volume of sound such as few who are not used to travelling in odd corners of Asia can imagine. Mounting my camel, I ride some hundred yards or so out of the crowd so that I may see the picture in its entirety.

From this distance I receive a much better impression of the caravan as a whole than when in its midst. At first, it gives the impression of a dull-bright mass of colour in which the primary hues—reds, blues, greens—predominate, with here and there a splash of gamboge or snowy white. The several races which make up the people of the pilgrimage are easily discovered. There are the dreamy-eyed, visionary men of Turkestan, the stalwart, soldierly Afghans, the placid Turks, the more volatile Egyptians, each in the garb of his community.

The caravan forms up into a long line of colour. The time has not yet come to cast off bright garments for the white and grey of the pilgrimage. As the sun climbs slowly upward it strikes on the garish pageant of our pious column, turning it into a flower garden. The guards, mounted on horseback, and with rifle on

7

knee, take their places at the head of the procession. The caravan is ready to start: only the smouldering fires are left in the sarai.

But then there occurred the usual delay. The caravan master must be interviewed by a hundred anxious folk as he rides from end to end of the column. Many of these people come from districts the most unfrequented, and are quite unused to travel. They are out of their environment, and cannot understand conditions. Their questions are not put very clearly, or are, perhaps, couched in a language unknown to the leader.

Others pray incessantly, hoping that this will add merit to their pilgrimage. Again and again they repeat their prayers or verses from holy literature. The clamour of their vociferation fills the ears like the drone of a myriad of bees; occasionally a voice, louder than the rest, rises above the hum.

Suddenly there is a roar from the front of the train. A pack-camel has run amok, has bitten the animal in front of it and kicked it in its rear. Uproar ensues. The owner of the beast is deluged with pious curses, and with much ado drags it by the halter out of the column.

A rifle-shot rolls over the plain in a series of reverberating echoes. It is the signal for departure. We are off. But it is slow progress at first. The camel is a beast which takes a long time to get under way. The digestion of his morning meal and the absorption of the large quantities of water he drinks before starting on a journey, occupy an unconscionable time, and until then he is likely to be surly and even wicked in temper. Those who know him best do not seek to chastise him, but to humour him, if possible—a difficult task. The rocking of the camel from side to side is like that of a boat on the sea, and occasionally has the same results.

The caravan, as seen by an outrider like myself, keeping clear of its flanks for some miles of its progress, has the appearance of a great coloured serpent as it winds over the desert sands. It seems a rainbow fallen flat to earth and moving slowly across the plain, and which, having no wings to bear it back to heaven, must crawl these sands until their golden dust heap over it and bury it deeply—until some poet finds it and by his magic restores it to the skies. On, on it drags, under the now merciless sun, constant prayers arising from its straggling ranks.

8

The Golden Caravan

In this brilliant column is packed all the romance and wonder of the East; it is the Arabian Nights in motion, an epitome of the marvels of the Orient. At night such tales are told around its camp-fires as a novelist would give years of life to hear, tales told by artists who are yet amateurs, life-histories of adventure in every land of Asia, adventure often so seemingly incredible that one not belonging to this wandering brotherhood would laugh aloud, could he follow its recital. But there is no laughter here. These bronze-faced listeners comprehend the nature of the artist's task, and know full well that few stories are worth the telling unless gilded by gorgeous words, and that, as like as not, they have an inner meaning. And again, the incredible does happen in the East, is happening there every day.

All day the caravan trails its length along the golden plain, slowly, but with all the certainty of fate. At the hour of sunset it halts, the *azan* is called and devotions are engaged in. Then the evening meal is prepared according to the strict regulations of pilgrimage and the several national customs of the pilgrims. The most extraordinary concoctions are made, the most extraordinary quantity of water is consumed.

There is very little sleep. All night long, pious and perfervid men repeat their prayers or texts incessantly. The staying-power of some of the aged patriarchs is enormous. They appear to be made of hammered steel. Neither the fierce solar rays, the lack of good water, hunger, nor the want of sleep affects them in the slightest degree. They rise in the morning, straight as poplars, fresh as palms in an oasis, with supplications on their bearded lips.

The caravan is the symbol of religious sacrifice. What inclusion in its ranks means to the devout cannot be said in mere words. In many cases it implies a lifetime's hoarding and strenuous toil, so that a man may behold the city of his desire. And for a season he becomes again the nomadic patriarch who lies behind the history of his faith and fervour—the man who walks in Allah's way.

Thuswise we had started on our long, long trail on the pilgrims' way: and, at the end of the day's journey, rested at another caravansarai.

Although none formed permanent groups or separate parties

9

within the caravan as such—as all men are one in the eyes of Allah—nevertheless some of us threw our worldly goods together as we rested at night: I was with a professor and a wandering merchant.

"He is sleeping, if ever a man slept," said the copper merchant to me, nodding towards a placid-faced man in the shade of the balcony of the sarai.

"No, my brother-in-faith," said I to the corpulent merchant, "the professor is like that always. I have often thought that he indulged in deep daydreams: but he merely meditates!"

"Leave alone, leave alone, sheik of sheiks!" whispered our camel-driver; "such men are better asleep, for they talk like books."

The three of us sat in a cell of that caravansarai in Old Istanbul, where, in days gone by, much merchandise passed to the lands of the West. Carpets from Bukhara, spice from Ind, salt and vinegar from Trabzon and goodly loads of dried fruit from Izmir were brought thither by a million lumbering camels.

But now its glory had faded. New routes, newer methods of carrying goods were in vogue, and we pilgrims were among the five guests in the old sarai that night.

The man whose trance was the subject of our remarks was no other than Sheik Ahmed Bey. He had written more books than he had read: and, in the lore of the ancient East, few equalled him.

Like me, a globe-trotter pilgrim, who sought nothing better from life but to bend his steps from shrine to shrine of Old Asia, from Holy Mecca, to Meshed Sharif, to Kerbala Moala, Bukhara Sharif and much further, the Professor of Philosophy was a pilgrim—a pilgrim not only in the sense of performing the sacred rites at Mecca, but a seeker who sought more than the outwardness of a green turban as the reward for his Haj to the sacred shrines.

The Professor's thoughts about diverse matters were so remarkable, and the methods and words which he chose to describe them so extraordinary, that to most men his speech at times was one long string of allegories.

The copper merchant, too, was somewhat of a philosopher: corpulent, with a healthy appetite, and a taste in dress so elegant as to be inconsistent with his pilgrim-calling that I once remarked to him about it. He was passionately fond of a mantle of green silk which always lay at his bedside, and which afterwards I persuaded him to sell to me: but thereby hangs a tale.

We shall hear of this garment later. But, this particular night, I suggested that we should pass the night before the dawn start in exchanging tales. The learned Professor, an Afghan from one of our noblest families, a wanderer and former military man who had lived in both the East and the West, agreed to start.

"My life, dear friends," he began, "is not of those who go to the moon—but I shall tell you of idealism and hard riding, of a fight and of an intrigue, in the days when I was still clear of eye and strong of arm.

I shall tell you of how things went for us in Central Asia."

ESCAPE FROM CENTRAL ASIA

Summer and Winter, said the Professor, I get up at six in the morning: but on that August day in the Afghan mountains, I had overslept. The night before had been rather disturbing, because of the earth tremors which often shake the uplands of this part of Central Asia in the Summer months.

Still, it was not as late as all that. And I was surprised to see that an Army officer had been waiting for me to rise; waiting on my veranda for over an hour and a half. He must have arrived soon after first light.

My servant ushered him in. Ramrod-stiff, he clicked his heels: "My orders are that you are to proceed immediately with me to the headquarters of the Governor, Sir."

The abruptness of the summons annoyed me not a little, for my feelings were mixed. Firstly, I outranked the man who had sent for me. Secondly, the lurking suspicion suffused my thoughts: was the cat out of the bag? Wedged between the might of British India southward and the advancing Bolshevist hordes to the north, idealist Afghans were anxious to do their bit to stem the Red tide. Thoughts began to form in my head. Had the intelligence officers at the Afghan capital of Kabul, southwards from my home, received urgent news of conditions in the Red lands across the River Oxus? In what way would such news affect the success or failure of our scheduled secret mission?

Intelligence material is a highly perishable commodity. Not being able to hold it, Headquarters might be trying to contact me before the rendezvous arranged for that afternoon. From a security point of view, using the usual channels of communication could be a serious mistake. My mountain retreat, miles from telephonic or telegraphic contact with the capital, at the end of a bridle path and watched by our sworn levies, had not been chosen from a whim. By the time I arrived at the Wali's office, I was boiling inside: curiosity and indignation was the mixture.

The Governor, however, had another story to tell me. A spy had been captured in the neighbourhood. Knowing that this might mean something to me, he had immediately made contact. Would I interrogate him? The Wali looked at me with that combined mixture of understanding and caution which is standard among the people of the Hindu Kush mountains.

"You might be able to tell us whether the matter should be reported to the higher-ups."

The suspect was tied to the trunk of an ancient tree which shaded the governor's yard. He was obviously in some pain, for the leather thongs of his bonds were cutting into his broad wrists, and he looked as though he had had a manhandling, and a rough one. Tall, blue-eyed and powerfully built, he had several days' growth of beard. His grey shirt and khaki trousers were the worse for wear. His reddish hair had not been combed for quite a time.

Some mountain farmers had had him under observation for several days. They had wondered why a man should swim three times a day: emerging from a cave and plunging into a hillside snow-fed burn, the water of which was almost too cold to drink—even for the average Afghan hillman. The farmers had first fed him for a few days, thinking him to be some sort of holy man from India: until someone told them that Indians did not have such fair skins. So they had seized him and turned him over to the governor of Paghman.

The first World War had ended in 1918, and it was now four years later. We Afghans, trained to the trigger, exulting in horsemanship and guarding our independence, were relatively cut off from the cross-currents of world affairs. Yet I knew that there were still a number of restless spirits from the War roaming in remote countries of the world; unanchored in their early life, seeking peace, money or adventure. Moving to some unknown destination, such men were not necessarily spies. Only our gigantic fear of the Russian steamroller and our present deep-laid plot made me partially sensitive.

I addressed the stranger in French, then in German, with little response. When I asked in English whether he was British or American his eyes narrowed, as if he did not want to divulge his nation's name; but as though he understood the language which I spoke. "He is from an English-speaking country," J concluded.

"You look like a brave man" I told him, "and we respect such people here. I am sure that neither you nor I should be ashamed of naming his own country!" He shook the hair out of his eyes, as if the remark had gone home.

"I am an American citizen!" he barked at me. "So what?"

His painful wrists were rubbed with healing ointment, and we gave him a chair to sit on, when the Governor, on my recommendation, had him released. Gratefully he drew on a cigarette. Then he spoke briefly. He was from the United States, had been soldiering during the late War. He was trying to forget war, thought of himself as a citizen of the world, and craved some meaningful adventure. As to the pretty face in the locket which he wore—well, that was his own business. I noted that the trinket had been made by a jeweller in Seattle.

All this I believed, but a few more enquiries had to be made before the authorities agreed to let Charles J. Ekar join me, as a 'person completely vindicated of the charge of espionage.'

It was determined at a conference that I was to discover if he was as efficient as he claimed in making ammunition; and, indeed, how loyal he might be to the cause for which we might badly need his services. It took me less than a week to make up my mind on both of these points. We were more than pleased to have an adventuring American in our mission, which involved two kings and a Turkish warlord on the one side; and the whole might of the Bolshevist forces of Eastern Turkestan on the other.

The time of which I narrate was of crucial importance. A wrong turning of events might well have altered the map of Asia during that late summer. Denniken was beaten, and the White Russian troops were in full flight. The Dunsterville Force of the British had no hope of retaining oil-rich Baku on the Caspian Sea. King Amanulla Khan, the young monarch of Afghanistan, had just emerged from the Third Afghan War, the sovereign ruler of a free people. Northwards of our country, the Emir of Bokhara had been driven out of his kingdom by the Bolsheviks and had been a political refugee in Kabul since 1920. Finally, Mahatma Gandhi was making things none too comfortable for the paramount power in India.

Asia was rocking. If the Reds could be stopped, well and good. But if they thought that they could overcome all resistence everywhere, they would sweep over the Middle East and much more. History showed this to be the Russian plan for centuries. The situation in Central Asia, threatened by the Soviets, needed stabilising. In Eastern Turkestan, the Basmachi Revolt among the Uzbeks seemed almost the only hope. It was led by the famous Turkish General Enver Pasha, one of the bravest men who ever lived. It was this revolt that we hoped to stiffen. We were in touch with the Pasha, who had been appointed Commander-in-Chief in the field by the exiled Emir of Bokhara. Enver was no stay-at-home general. He had gone from Turkey to the land of his fathers, Turkestan, to win or die.

Under the shadow of these events of world importance a group of us met soon after Ekart's appearance in the Afghan capital to plan how to render help in men, skill and money to the resistance leaders, who were ill-equipped and yet straining to give relentless battle to any coloniser. To us, the threat was Communism. All the Uzbeks, however, wanted was their freedom: they did not care who threatened it, Czarist or Red. They now have a Communist State; but that was something which had no relevance to us at that time. There was still a chance.

The Emir of Bokhara was financing the resistance movement from a treasure of some 125 million dollars worth of gold which he had smuggled out of his country into ours. Volunteer horsemen from Afghan-Turkestan in the north, seasoned warriors all, were being sent in batches of three and four hundred to join Enver Pasha and his men, or to Enver's ally, the Basmachi leader Ibrahim Beg, in the Tajik Mountains of Turkestan. Ours was the fourth—and as it happened the last—contingent to go.

Moscow had pressed the Afghan king, asking how a resistance movement could properly be conducted from Afghanistan, when its king was in friendly relations with the Soviets. Amanullah Khan answered that he, as head of the Government, was not conducting the campaign. Islamic law made sanctuary to refugees and holy warriors a sacred duty. Neither did the Government of Afghanistan have anything to do with it. The Emir of Bokhara was paying for the struggle out of his own money; the tribal volunteers were independent fighting-men over whom the Afghan throne had no control. Lenin had to be satisfied with this.

It was the fateful Thursday when we were to have our final briefing, and then to start for the unknown situation in Turkestan. Present at the meeting at Chihil Sutoun Palace were the two kings: Amanullah Khan of Afghanistan and the Emir of Bokhara. Others included the Chief of Afghan Intelligence, the Commander of the Uzbeks, Charles Ekar, two master gun-makers from the unruly Pathan Frontier of India, and myself as leader of the expedition.

My qualifications included the fact that I had lived in Europe and during previous enterprises I had met General Enver Pasha and the 'Hero of the Mountains', Ibrahim Beg. So I 'knew the state of the crops', as we say in our language. I also spoke several local dialects. Considered something of a renegade, by imperialists and Marxists alike, I had been campaigning in three continents for the right of every people to sovereign nationhood. What personal risk such an activity involved fifty years ago can only really be appreciated by those, in East and West, who were incarcerated for breathing such an idea. We were not always right: but that put us in good company. . .

As soon as our conclave started the Emir of Bokhara rose to address us. What was this novel idea? Previously we had always sat around a large oval table, made brief reports, and decided upon the next step.

The Emir harangued us on what was known as 'Pan-Turanism'. There was, he said, a great population of Turkic origin in his realm. This had been detached from the great Empire of the Ottomans in Asia Minor. It must now be re-united. In a few minutes, he left us in no doubt that he was envisaging a mighty empire of all the Turks—the Grand Turkic Empire. And there should be a King at the head of it.

Since there was now no more hope for a strong Sultan of Turkey, it was obvious that the Bokhara Emir saw himself cast in the role of Grand Turk, a new and mightier Sultan.

I was not prepared for this, and Charles Ekar gave me a look as much as to say that I had perhaps tricked him into throwing in his lot with us; for I had spoken of a different cause.

The Afghan king, too, was rather surprised. The Turkestani officer was restless, thinking of the lives of his comrades which were at that very moment being lost across the Oxus for want of our help. He told his king to sit down and stop talking nonsense. The Afghan Intelligence chief begged the Emir to 'give up the gold and let us proceed to battle' for, as he stressed, Enver Pasha and Ibrahim Beg were anxiously awaiting us.

There was no time to lose, it transpired from the intelligence picture, for Kolesov's men might even now be converging upon Eastern Turkestan. Time was more than precious. We must leave that very night to catch up with the men of the escort who had been instructed to give protection to our caravan, while the remaining horsemen were starting from northern Tashkurghan towards the Oxus. We had no time for political arguments, for reorientating our mission to dovetail with an empire-making plan. We were helping the national movement of the Uzbeks, not catering for personal whims. Idealism, some of us realised at that time, not gain, was our motive.

The conference was becoming overcharged with conflicting ideals. "Everything that goes into a salt mine, becomes salt" spat the Bokharan king. "I have been doling out my gold in donkey-loads: and yet my throne is as far distant as it ever has been in the past two years." He seemed to want to make some sort of a pact with us as a condition of his paying out any more. He continued that he had been fooled by two adventurers, Enver and Ibrahim. The Turkish general might have a great reputation in ridiculous European wars; what had he done in Turkestan? He had grown a beard, oh yes, and donned Tajik clothes. Had Enver ever said a prayer in his life . . . and what about . . ? He was going to ask the modernistic Afghan King the same question. At that juncture King Amanullah Khan also lost his temper.

"A man need not be a Mecca pilgrim to fight for a people" he growled. "What has all this got to do with the Emir handing over his gold? Let the Mission proceed. Or else . . ."

"Or else *what?*" barked the Bokharn.

At this I threw Court etiquette to the winds and shouted:

"Or else, Emir, you will be flung out of Afghanistan, minus your gold!"

The Emir slumped. He knew, of course, that if he were

17

expelled from Afghanistan there was nowhere else that he could go. He had already offered his kingdom to the British in India as soon as he fled his own capital. Finding the load of India itself rather heavy upon their shoulders, it has been supposed, they refused the kind offer. Two days before this meeting, the Emir had raised a laugh when be proposed that I induce Charles Ekar to return to America to enrol Uzbekistan as one of the Sovereign States of the U.S.A. He was full of ideas.

The Turkestani patriot clenched his great fists. The veins stood out on his forehead. His wife and female children were in Uzbekistan. His sons were somewhere in the mountains, with perhaps only their bare hands to use against the enemy. I felt that if he spoke another word, King of Afghanistan present or not, Jinabi-Aali His High Presence Mir Alam Khan, Emir of Bokhara and her Dependencies would receive a Turkestani fist bang in his face.

Glowering, the Emir handed over his keys to his treasure-house in Wazirabad, not far from Kabul. The matching set, without which the doors could not be opened, we had literally to wrench from the hands of his treasurer, the Diwan Begi, who tried to refuse them to us without a written paper. "But I cannot give anyone anything without a *parcha*, a paper," he moaned. "The enemy will take your land without a *parcha*, pardner," said Charles as he spat on the ground at the cowering courtier's feet.

Seventy troopers soon filled the coins into stout leather bags, together with a quantity of rice to disguise the contents, and to stop the chink of metal.

By daybreak we were on the northern road to Charikar. The incline started fairly early on our way to Kotal Khair Khana. This is the border between Kabul and the northern province, where we had little difficulty in pushing onwards with our 'rice caravan' because the officer in charge there had his instructions to give all facilities to our group. He offered us green tea, hospitality and much else, none of which we wanted, for a forced march was our aim. Before sundown we managed to cover twelve miles to our first halt at the little village of Fort Murad Beg, which was rather confusing because some of the locals called it this, while others said its name was Hussain Kot.

Here we bought fresh fruit, available in abundance, and

luxuriated while we could, the tensions of the Mission somewhat compensated by the rations. Grapes of all kinds were less
than one penny a pound, peaches, mulberries and apricots
practically given away. We used them both as food and drink
for the night's repast.

A little before dawn the next day we started, after a short
conference. We had to make a real effort to cover the next thirty
miles or so to Charikar before nightfall. And there were two
very stiff climbs at over seven thousand and nine thousand feet
above sea-level on the way to Sarai Khwaja and Qarabagh.
After that there would be a rough descending road to Charika.
At any point on the ascent we might be attacked by bandits,
the free-ranging badmen who called these mountains their
own domain.

Bandits did not worry Charles much, and he pointed out that
if we were not ambushed, he might have time to see an ancient
Buddhist stupa in the neighbourhood, where he thought might
be hidden relics of the Buddha himself. And, he said, there
might be treasure buried there. We had enough gold as it was,
and more perhaps than we might be able to deliver. But
Charles had read somewhere—he turned out to be a great
amateur archaeologist as well as everything else—that among
the relics there might be scrolls. "Those scrolls" he said, in his
slow way, "could contain remedies for many illnesses. These
should be given to the whole civilised world." Was he a doctor
too?

Half the caravan train had already climbed the high pass
when our American bag-of-tricks dug in his toes and insisted
that he have time to explore the neighbourhood. We decided to
stop for the night at Sarai Khwaja, and Charles went off on a
reconnaissance. When he returned a little later, sure enough,
he had some curious little terra-cotta figurines in his hand. I
was too tired to take much interest. I ate bread made from
mulberry-flour and had a gulp of snow-cooled water before
turning in.

It could not have been much past midnight when a
tremendous hue and cry struck my ears. The whole caravan-
serai was in an uproar: *"Begir o naman!"* (get him and don't let
go!)—"here he is!" and so on. Here and there in the nearby
mulberry grove shots were fired. The entire population of the

19

place seemed to fill the serai. Men were holding oil torches aloft; others were brandishing clubs, ploughshares: anything that could be used as a weapon. In the confusion I could not make out our men from the strangers who were, it seemed, attacking us.

In the centre of a spinning knot of human flesh and bone I saw the fists of Charlie rising and falling. Soon I was in the middle of the fray, hitting out at anyone who struck at me. Men scattered on every side, formed and rallied.

Two of our men had thrown themselves upon the American to prevent any more blows reaching him. One of the officers blew a harsh blast on his whistle and his men detached themselves from the struggle and rallied to him. In this way they left the interlopers exposed at the far wall of the Serai. Our very resourceful officer switched on a searchlight. He had already posted a firing-party beside him, and now he ordered them to shoot at whoever was illuminated by the lamp. Five fell dead, others were wounded, about thirty fled through the open doors of the great building.

On cease-fire we found that Charlie had a gash on his right thigh. A long, Afghan killing-knife lay beside him. He was calmly bandaging himself with a rolled turban, with the quiet skill of a physician.

The alertness and effiency of our officers had beaten off an attack by a powerful band of brigands. Some of them had managed to escape with two sacks of our 'rice'.

"This is what comes of giving tips to all and sundry when you go off hunting Buddhist relics," I said to Charles, rather uncharitably. He was more concerned with the lost gold than with his wound. "Two loads means the wages of six hundred fighting-men, didn't you say?", he asked me, with pain in his eyes.

It took all my persuasive powers to make him get into his sleeping bag. "We shall see about that in the morning," I said. Mounting a double watch, I dozed off.

Soon I woke with a start to see that Charles had shed his sleeping-bag and was gone. How, for the love of goodness, was I to find a conscience-smitten American in the blackness of an Afghan pre-dawn night, on a wild mountain?

Find him I must, I thought. His skill in many fields, as well as his friendship now that we were all in complete sympathy and understanding, was worth more than his weight in gold. He might be murdered in the night, he might lose his way. A search for him would certainly delay our start in the morning.

Then, as if from nowhere, appeared Charles again. He unbuckled his crossed cartridge bandoliers, took his two revolvers from his cummerbund—and lay down without a word. In a few minutes he said: "It's all right. I have the bags back. They are O.K. The two men who were trying to open them are dead, though."

I sat up and shone my flashlight on him. "Dead, how?" was all I could think of saying. He just pointed to his guns, to his fist, and to another flesh-wound on his arm: and reminded me that within two hours we must be starting off again. Then we made a pact that, come what may, he would not seek further Buddhist secret remedies, whatever the loss to the medicaments of the civilised world.

We were soon in a veritable paradise of a land, which seemed so remote from the grim realities of the life-and-death struggle ahead that I constantly reminded myself of the differences. Even before one reaches Sarai Khwaja, Northern Afghanistan is a garden of a place. Mountain rills of ice-cold water, trees burdened with fruits of all kinds, little hamlets and every sign of abundance make a picture difficult to match. But, having a job on hand, we did not allow ourselves to 'pluck the flowers at the wayside', as the Afghan idiom has it. Therefore we started early to tackle the Qarabagh road.

We had to skirt the passes of over nine thousand feet by nightfall: a trial in mountain climbing with our overloaded animals which might have daunted anyone. We were constantly being challenged by problems of negotiation which in themselves would have constituted a severe test of endurance.

It was a killing pace, with even our hardened men getting mountain sickness. At the same time, my officers and I were often sustained by the glow of pride which we felt in the unswerving loyalty of our men, who never once questioned an order. In fact, they often even anticipated the commands which we had to give them. They knew that great events were at stake. At Charikar I expected another message from beyond the Oxus. If it did not tell of defeat, it would say, we knew, that even

21

more urgency was the watchword.

It was just as well that we did arrive in Charikar at the dead of night. This fair-sized town at the crossroads of east, north and western Afghanistan was agog with expectations. Presents were expected by every inhabitant—and from whom? From the Soviet Delegation, which was making its way to the Afghan capital from Moscow. This so-called commercial mission had arrived in town the same afternoon. They were not strong enough to fight us, I found out, because in sovereign Afghanistan they were precluded as foreigners from carrying arms. Even so, we realised that if they knew too much about us, they might have ways and means; at least of sending messages somewhere that we were to be intercepted.

In a few short hours the Delegation had won for themselves the name of *Mahbuba* (Beloved) because they had handed out to five hundred men and women a silk handkerchief each and a pound of candy: from 'friends in the Sovietland'. Since they were guests of the Afghan king, the people were well disposed towards them. If they had not been received as guests, the chips might have been down. And at this point there was still no accurate information circulating as to their evil intentions. The Mulla of the Friday Mosque had been invested with a silken green turban and seven gold pieces, a 'present from the Rector of the Muslim Theological School of Bokhara'—a Rector who was probably lying somewhere, very dead. Our would-be friends were rather good at public relations.

In the circumstances we considered that it might be as well not to put up at the same caravansarai as the visitors. In the end we had to bivouac in a mulberry grove just inside the town. Our presence seems to have been known, though our purpose perhaps was not. A well-mounted caravan of battle-tough soldiers with iron discipline was probably up to something. . .

Hardly had we pitched our felt tents when a messenger arrived—from a quite unknown merchant—asking whether we wanted any fresh fruit or cheese, for which the place is famous.

This might have been merely incidental, but we were able to take no chances. The visit was reported to the Wali of Charikar. Fortunately he had received instructions to look after us, by a fast-travelling, unladen, secret messenger. The result was that the merchant's servant was seized and given treatment designed to ascertain whether he was in fact a spy. We did not pursue the question of his fate, and left Charikar early in the morning.

After a few miles of desolate rocks we arrived at the Ghorband river. An iron bridge was being built across its turbulent waters, and we had to decide upon more ancient methods of crossing. We could wait our turn on the ferry raft, or swim it, or use goatskin floats called *mushaks* to get across. The raft was too rickety; especially as its floor, of decaying straw, would not sustain our animals' hooves. But, we decided, a number of horseman could swim across, leading the animals with the help of the buoyancy given by inflated skins.

Our particular anxiety were the ammunition-packs and pieces of equipment. The barrels of rifles could not be folded, and protruded out of the 'rice sacks'. Small-arms machinery was difficult to disguise. Cartridges had to be placed on the men's heads to keep them dry. And a full cartridge box is no joke to carry on one's head, while paddling an inflated goatskin with the other hand; holding the box secure and yet keeping in full balance on an ever-wobbling inflated skin in a swift-running current. "This would wow them at a Chinese circus" panted Charles, beside me.

We had several cases of duckings, but not a single cartridge box was lost. Three men who were practically at drowning-point held on to their loads with superhuman tenacity, until others, themselves scarcely able to keep upright, jostled them against the supporting buoyancy of the elusive, slippery skins.

I never knew that Charles had so much armour on his person, until I saw him on a swimming pony with a bulbous sack of personal armaments perilously poised on his head. He was also directing the third wave of troopers like a very efficient cavalry sergeant-major.

But worse troubles, if that is possible, were to begin when we reached the internal Customs post on the other bank of the river. True, King Amanullah Khan was a ruler with very advanced views on administration. But his orders were not penetrating to every nook and cranny of the kingdom with the efficiency which he would have desired. Up to Charikar, everyone had expedited our journey. Here, only a few miles further on, nobody had heard of us. We were treated as a very suspicious caravan, probably smugglers. This was a Customs check-post inside Afghan territory, not even on a border.

We had the most imposing documents; permits to travel, identity documents signed by the two Kings in their own hand, and the necessary insignia of top-ranking military officers on special Mission. The illiterate officer of the Customs tried, desultorily, to show his intelligence by looking at some of these pieces of paper and metal upside-down.

He looked at us through his one good eye.

"Who are you?"

"It is all in these papers" shouted the Turkestani Commander.

"*I* am the one who decides how to test you!" roared the idiot, revelling in his power.

We told him more or less who we were.

" You are pitching it a little too high" he snarled, "your claims are just too much. Oh, yes, I admit that you're up to something. But I don't think it is with any of the high-ranking blessings you claim."

"I can have you hanged!" I told him.

"For doing my duty?"

"You can't do your duty if you can't read or write, and if you can hardly think!" shouted one of our gunsmiths, a massive Pathan warrior who, true to his kind, loathed all forms of officialdom.

On our refusal to bandy words with him any further, the Customs man ordered his small group of men to be ready to fire at us; and to shoot if we even moved. We had been inching towards him during the heat of the discussion. I suggested that one of his men might accompany one of ours to Charikar, to determine our bona-fides, if his own telephone was not working. He was clearly both out of his depth and very stubborn. I repeated the request as soon as he had shaken his head. He had, he said, only seven men at this post, and we outnumbered him by hundreds. He could not afford to weaken his force; especially if we were going to attack the post, which was what he expected us to do.

Through the paneless window of the mud-hut office I saw that the American had edged his way outside and given an order to our troopers. They were dismounted and standing by their horses. Charles must be arranging some sort of a *coup*. Suddenly I heard him whistle softly. This was a signal pre-arranged between us all. It meant:"Ready to fire. Fire at the second whistle".

The Turkestani officer had also seen this. And then things began to happen.

The Turkestani, swinging round upon the Customs officer, upset the table over him, hurling him to the ground, his revolver spinning away into a corner. The first Afghan officer, a huge bear of a man, grabbed him as he scrambled for his gun. They reached it together, and it went off, the bullet hitting the ceiling. The Customs men outside the hut discharged a volley, ostensibly at our men, but in reality into the air. No fools they, they knew what might happen to them if they hit any of our battle-hardened toughs. At the same time—for the look of it—they had to make some move.

Our men held their fire. Charles had not given his second whistle. Standing beside his mount he seemed to be rather enjoying the fun. The Customs man was soon bound and gagged; his men, calling him *'diwana'* (Madman) anxiously assured us that they disliked him and did not want to go to his help.

Then we gave this insolent man a good eight lashes on his behind; and, having put him in his own lockup and leaving a note for the officer in charge of Charikar, we resumed our course. We had wasted quite enough time in wrangling with this fool. I heard later that he was soundly beaten at Customs Headquarters at Kabul for that day's work. He should have confirmed our credentials with the local military H.Q.

Soon we were following the course of the Gharband River westwards, through an undulating fairyland of orchards, mountain streams and vineyards. Neat little houses are dotted here and there among the fruit trees and for ten miles we saw an orchard of ripening fruit. Life seemed good again, and our spirits rose as we began to think that rescue, after all, might come partly through our hands, to the freedom-fighters of Turkestan. People came out onto their rooftops to look at us as they heard the mighty roar of our war-songs: an unrehearsed chorus of such volume that groups of farmers cheered—without knowing why—when they were engulfed in wave upon wave of

25

the immemorial bass chant "Youth into Battle" of our conquering ancestors.

Towards the evening we reached Farinjal village, a small place at the bottom of a climb of about seven thousand feet above sea-level, to arrive at the townlet of Chahardeh Gharband after midnight.

This halt was made all the more necessary because three of our pack-ponies were limping, and this was the point at which a despatch-carrier from Eastern Turkestan was scheduled to make contact with us. And we had ahead of us the stiff climb of Shibar Kotal, rising to nearly ten thousand feet, before we were to descend into Daray Shikari, Hunter's Valley, where a bend had to be negotiated in our route from the west to regain our northward course.

Here at Chahardeh Gharband a great feast awaited us, arranged by the local Governor. His lines of communication, at any rate, were working well; and he awaited us. We sat around huge platters of roast fat-tailed sheep, mountains of rice, many bunches of grapes and dishes of green almonds. In those days we ate like giants. We were in superb physical condition, enduring circumstances which would have been impossible at the earlier stages of our trek.

The American fell victim to this feast. He was not a whit behind the ravenous troopers in his appetite; but the combination of the fresh juice of grapes with almonds—especially when their husks were still green—produced an unhappy chemical mixture which was liable to give an acute stomach-ache to people not used to it. Charles was rather badly affected by it, and writhed with pain until he got rid of what he had eaten. We gulped gallons of cardamom-spiced tea with cream floating upon it, the delicious *Qaimagh Chai*, and in spite of our fatigue, gave an impromptu concert of the haunting melodies of the mountains before slumping into a dreamless sleep.

In the morning Charles was still not too well, but he would not think of staying behind to recover. "If I let you guys out of my sight, there is no telling what you might get up to," he laughed. In a few minutes after setting out that crisp morning I saw him leading his part of the train as nonchalantly as if he had grown on the saddle.

We were not sorry to leave the place, in spite of the

hospitality of the Governor. We soon discovered that vast portions of the area stank of assafoetida, which grows abundantly here, and is exported to Peshawar, to the far south, where it is used as a meat preservative in hot weather.

Hardly three miles up the first hill we came upon the exhausted messenger from Eastern Turkestan. His difficulties in getting through to us would itself make an epic. But, as he said, "I got here. Now you get there!" He was a tough Mongol of few words.

As we really already knew in our hearts, the situation was more than critical. "Hurry," was Enver's message, "or all will be lost." The bottle-neck produced by the patriot armies to the north of Do-Shambay (later renamed Stalin-abad) had been burst open by vastly superior forces of the Red Army. The tribal levies, some of them unreliable, would desert unless money were forthcoming to pay them. They felt that if the situation was crumbling, they would do better out of loot than soldiering for a lost cause. The quality of the local fighting-man varied enormously, and the patriots just had to make use of whatever material they could muster.

Despite the great prestige of the tribal leader Ibrahim Beg, the Tajiks on the whole preferred to side with the winners. The Nationalist Cause could fend for itself.

This grave news did not allow us to slow down our precipitous ascent of Shibar Kotal (10,000 feet high) and we pressed on. The next stage was to curve towards the north. We hastened as fast as ever possible into the valley beyond Shibar Kotal, where the track—for it was little more—wound through hairpin bends, and bend within bends, following the contours of the rocks.

Crossing the Bamyan road (I did not tell Charles that there were two immense rock-carved standing Buddhas there, though perhaps he would not have cared by now) we had to pass over rickety bridges in a nightmare of apprehension for our men and pack animals. Very late at night we arrived at out northernmost point, Mekh-i-Zarin.

Taking stock of our condition, we realised that this was the hardest forty miles that any one of us had ever done. No less than twenty-one ponies had to be destroyed on the way due to lameness or accident. Their loads had been redistributed on the remaining pack-animals and the horses of our troopers. The first priority now was to buy more animals.

It was obvious to the local farmers that we needed these beasts very badly. They also sensed that we would pay anything for them. There was no other source of supply; they had us where they wanted us. There was not even time for the traditional bargaining. Ordinarily, the price was no more than 150 dollars an animal. We had to give them a little over eight hundred dollars each, and that in the fine deep yellow gold of Bokhara. What was gold, we asked ourselves, when the fate of thirty million people might hang on the balance of our progress?

Our road troubles, we thought, were probably over. Although I had not travelled this route to Turkestan before, I understood that we could now make a fairly easy march north-eastward to Doshi. The road lay along the banks of the river, which we had to cross and recross several times by the same method as we had used earlier, on inflated goatskins and beam-floats.

Having rid ourselves of the incredible Afghan mountain system, we could even trot the ponies a little on the plain of Doshi, in the hope of covering forty miles. But as soon as we emerged from our resting-place, we came upon train after train of camels, loaded with coal from the western road, leading to the Ash Pushta mines. They barred our way for hours. The entire camel population of the world, it seemed to us at times, was taking coal to the Afghan capital. We made it, however, by midnight, and that night even the ubiquitous Turkestani mosquito did not keep us awake.

Next morning we covered the twenty-odd miles of fairly level road in an exact northerly direction to the now-industrialised area of Puli-Khumri, and pushed on to the plains of Haybak, on the banks of the river Khilm. Here we had no time to look at the ancient ruins, some say of 5000 B.C., of ancient Aryana.

Now we hied forth to Tashkurghan through hilly land; and the next day we were glad to be at Mazari Sharif, the Holy Shrine of Ali, where we had to rest for two whole days. This was in order to divide the party into two. One proceeded towards Samarkand (Bokhara was already in Red hands) via the Oxus ferry at Kilif; and the other eastwards to Termez. All of our escorts, except five, were to go straight to render what assistance they could to rescue Bokhara, as a counter-attack was planned. The two Afghan officers were to lead them.

The gunmakers, the American and I were to proceed by way of Termez over the Oxus, with money, munitions apparatus and ammunition to Eastern Turkestan, where Enver Pasha was involved in very heavy fighting.

Unhappily, Fate decreed otherwise than a storming of great Bokhara for our doughty troopers. Thirsting for a fight, they got it before they bargained for it. They were liquidated by a massive attack by Bolshevist sympathisers as they crossed the river Oxus, like earlier contingents sent out by us. Our little party, following the Surkhab route, reached Do-Shambay just in time to stop and rally a number of tribal deserters. The picture looked grimmer than ever.

Ultimately, we made contact with the relentless Enver, a man of iron who held his men together by the sheer force of his tremendous personality. Some were patriots, others needed his constant rallying. The American soon started a field factory for the making and repair of light arms. Enver was satisfied that he was a real find. The money put stiffening into the picture, and reports coming into headquarters indicated that regrouping patriots were hurrying to our aid. Without the military genius of Enver, these wild but impractical men could do very little against a superior enemy. After the disasters of the past, it seemed, Enver's prestige and ability to stand and fight had impressed the Turkestanis, albeit sporadically, with the notion that he was a man in whom they must put their trust. Was it too late? I asked the evening sky. Here we were in the melting-pot of Turkestan, with history in the making.

Here in Do-Shambay, we pored over the situation reports, collated information, sent dispatches to all known resisting groups. Enver decided to weld the bits and pieces of Turkestan resistance into a force which might sweep Bolshevism, once and for all, out of Central Asia. Then another sort of news started to reach us. The twin nationalist leader—Ibrahim Beg—was plotting against Enver. Within a few days, the tide was turning in his favour. He had stigmatised Enver Pasha, the only real leader we had, as a foreigner, a Turk from Turkey, a refugee trying to carve out a kingdom for himself. Tribal men who had drawn their pay in gold from us and who owed any form of allegiance to Ibrahim deserted *en masse,* and with their arms.

Soon Do-Shambay was surrounded by Red forces.

Enver Pasha seemed determined to give battle. Charles and his other advisers, looking at the overall situation, talked him out of it. There was no point, we felt, in committing suicide. This would not serve the nationalist cause.

Reluctantly that night we retreated to high ground. Charles had already dismantled his little factory and sent it on ahead. I accompanied Enver with our remaining war-chest: eight donkey-loads of gold. How many men we had with us was unclear from time to time. As we moved towards the Afghan frontier, men were deserting at almost every step.

Ibrahim Beg had now definitely proclaimed himself the Head of the National Basmachi Movement, openly denouncing Enver, and specifically recalling his Lokai tribesmen. The other erstwhile important chief, Faizullah, also withdrew his forces, mouthing the lie that Enver wanted to be ruler of Bokhara. His men fled to Karategin, and we retreated to Kuliab, intending to make a comeback if at all possible, after consolidating our position. Time might help to clear the picture and restore confidence in Enver. As a military chief he had found himself implicated in political intrigue, and his task was even then seriously undermined by this distressing development.

At Baljuan, Enver addressed us all. As many tribal men as would listen were mustered, our own group, and those who were determined to do or to die. Enver proposed a last pitched battle, a battle in which our future would be decided.

"Fight for our Motherland, fight. . ." he shouted, "and do not let them divide up the homeland of our Turkish-speaking people. Can you cut up a cow and then hope to get milk from her?" He was hoarse with emotion, tears rolled down his cheeks. I had never seen him like this. This was the last desperate effort to save the Central Asians from becoming a subject people. If it failed, they would remain captives for fifty or a hundred years.

Before he could say another word, Charles hastened to us with the news that even as he was speaking, the Communists were mounting the other side of the hill on which we stood.

When moonlight was still available, we decided, we would stand and fight.

Enver gave the order; "Dear Friends—this is our battle-cry: Ride and die!"

We took our white death-shrouds and wrapped them as turbans around our heads: the final sign of the Moslem warrior that he was no longer interested in life on the enemy's terms. We formed up behind General Enver Pasha, the *Ghazi* (Hero), our hero. He stood in the stirrups of his white charger, his cavalry sword raised aloft: we heard his great voice calling— "Come to Battle!"

We drew our swords and moved silently down the hill: a handful against—how many?

A shower of bullets whined past, some of them apparently from automatic weapons. My horse fell under me, my head hit the rocks, floating stars filled my brain. I lost consciousness.

The actual battle took place all around me, as I lay there half pinned down by the carcase of the animal, pot-shotting with my revolver in the moonlight. The American, trying to shield Enver, was hit more than once. He rolled down a rock and slumped beside me. Moaning men with shattered limbs were trying to right themselves, or merely lying there silently. The struggle was fierce, and our men were giving as good as they got—and better. Enver was hit, at last.

The patriots were slashing and shouting like maniacs, here and there a grim duel, man to man, hand to hand, took place as the moon flitted in and out of the clouds. The Reds suddenly had had enough. Not knowing their victory, they retreated.

In the alternating light and dark of the moonlight, Charles and I limped among the dead and dying, looking for Enver. He lay in a pool of blood, his body riddled with bullets and we put him under a cairn of stones, saluting him for the martyr that he was.

At first light, Charles Ekar and I, together with eight other wounded men, crossed the Oxus river into Afghanistan, the entire remnant of a great mission.

When about to leave our country after his wounds were healed, I half-jokingly asked my American comrade whether we should go to fight for Turkestan again. We exchanged long looks, for the iron was in our souls. He was game enough, but I

31

knew what he thought before he said it. "I will go to battle in any clean fight. Against treachery, who can fight?"

The story of our last stand, and the manner of Enver's death, has passed into legend. It is still repeated, as are the ancient tales of chivalry and sacrifice, throughout the Turkic lands of Asia, free and enslaved alike. Perhaps it is too much to think that in this small measure we had not failed. For we had shown that men would still die for their beliefs in that part of the world. In death, Enver may have given that stiffening to parts of still-free Central Asia which he hoped to provide in life.

It was a real wrench to part with such a gallant companion in our cause as was Charles Ekar. But we had to say goodbye in our hills and glens of Paghman, where our mission had begun.

"Are you going back to the States?" I asked. "Maybe yes, maybe no. And by the way, my name is not Charles Ekar!" I cannot tell here his true name, however.

Later we were to go on another mission together. That, however, as Kipling would have said, is another story. But do not take us as spies and 'interventionists'—only mad idealists!

*   *   *

When the reverend gentleman with the white hair had finished his tale, we remained silent for some time, each absorbed in his own thoughts.

Then the Leader of the Caravan, one of the two Imams who accompanied us, cleared his throat.

"In all history there is allegory, and all allegory finds its expression in the lives of men. Therefore I take this story in both senses in which it can be understood.

"But the Learned One's recital is such that I would like to contribute something shorter, containing promise as well as admonition; something which happened to a certain man of this very city, who met the one known in the legend as The Rose of Istanbul."

THE ROSE OF ISTANBUL

Seyd Effendi (said the Imam), was a very happy young man because he knew the meaning of beauty: for when a man realizes this he cannot be otherwise than happy. He always wore a smile, a rather secret-seeming smile, which gave people to think he was frivolous. But like all real worshippers of the divinity of loveliness, he was as serious at heart as a man of sixty who knows that he is the only prop of a large family.

Seyd was but twenty-three, but already he had three wives. These had been thrust upon him by family and political exigencies. His first wife, Zara, was six years older than he, a large, over-sensible woman. Ayesha, the second, had been the young widow of a wealthy and childless pasha who had left her everything, and such a prize Seyd's mother could not resist for him. Danäe was a Greek, a prisoner in the last rebellion, given him by his General as a reward. He could not refuse her, and his idea of chivalry denied any other arrangement save marriage.

He had wished for none of these women, all three had been thrust upon him. They were content enough, but although he was kind, considerate and friendly with all three, he cared for none of them. He cared only for the beauty of the spiritual. He told himself that his temperament was that of the Sufi, one of those poet-mystics whose inner if not outward lives are given over to the ecstasy of the contemplation of the divine.

But this evening, as he stepped towards his barge through the most beautiful garden on the banks of the Golden Horn, Seyd realized that the hermitage was really unnecessary to ecstatic thinking and living. Here was Paradise at his very gate. Through the white columns of the Byzantine ruins standing where the garden met the sea, glowed the island-bearing sapphire of the Bosphorus, a plane of light beneath a turquoise sky dashed with thin gold. The linaments on the marble capitals were clear as in the sculptor's thought, and the stony wreaths of ivy, myrtle and pine which clustered the shattered pillars seemed not to move and grow only because no wind vexed the night's first rapture. It was good to live, not for vitality's sake but for the sake of that essence of the seraphic which drenches the airs of that golden place.

The light barge, under the compelling hands of its four black rowers, thrust its nose towards the jutting lands which almost meet at the bay's entrance. Seyd lit a *chibuq* and lay back in the cushions, taking in the magic of the evening. A frail drift of opal cloud held the upper sky, and the stars through this gazed as women's eyes through veiling.

Women's eyes! He smiled rather bitterly. To him there had at times seemed as much of devil as angel in womanhood. They were not serene, he felt: they had no depths of mind or soul, they were prone to obsessions and gross superstitions which clung to them like weed to the body of a ship. They were spirits of impulse, hating and loving in a breath. Allah alone knew why He had created them. Foolish men were captured by their little coquetries, but wise men avoided the snare of them, as they kept clear of all that was not good for the soul's life, he mused.

The barge shot through the harbour's mouth, and continued its course round the coastal fringe of silver sand lying without the Horn. The heaped miracle of Istanbul rose behind him, a mountain of minarets and rainbow domes, lofting into the illimitable turquoise of the Eastern night. At the spectacle of it, beautiful as a wreck of Paradise, his eyes overflowed with tears. When Nature and Man set hands to the same canvas what, with the aid of Allah, could they not achieve?

The barge drew shoreward, and toward a small jetty. Seyd landed, and told the crew to wait. He walked inland by a narrow path, plunging into a little wood where a small, ruined mosque stood in deserted whiteness. Although it was roofless and long deserted, although the murmur of prayer seldom ascended here, Seyd piously removed his peaked shoes before he entered. Some rainwater, limpid as aquamarine, lay in the shattered basin, and in this he made his ablutions.

Seating himself on one of the tilting flagstones, he began to pray, devoutly, utterly oblivious of his surroundings. This indeed was life, this communion with the Merciful, the Compassionate, Sultan and Sovereign of the Universe, of the seas and the stars, of men and of angels. The power of the

Divine seemed to interpenetrate every fibre of him, overflowing into his spirit in mystical golden rapture, making his heart blossom in love and the comprehension of heaven. He could understand how the Patriarchs and Prophets who walked with God had endured material existence but for such moments as this, which brought a sense of the everlasting beauty and nobility of the bond betwixt God and man. This was indeed life, joy, victory!

A slight noise behind him disturbed his devotions. He turned his head. He rose quickly. Before him in the gathering shadows which fell like thick curtains upon the little mosque stood a woman, heavily veiled. A sudden resentment seized him. To behold a woman there and at such an hour seemed monstrously inappropriate. Some crone, doubtless, who, with the privilege of age, came there to make secret invocations. Then he saw by her bare feet, white as alabaster, that she was a young woman. It was not right that he should be here alone with her. He would go.

But as he made to do so, he found his way barred by a shapely arm.

"Stay, Seyd," she said in a deep, rich voice that thrilled him in the deepest places of his blood. "Stay, for I am the answer to your prayer."

Amazed, he could scarcely speak. "How, lady?" he stammered. "I seem to know you, but . . ." Then the truth of the matter rushed in upon him. This was some woman of love, some courtesan who had tracked him here, seeking to beguile him and bring him to shame, a ghoul, perhaps, sent by Eblis to destroy him, soul and body.

"Let me pass," he said sternly. Her answer was to raise her veil, and at the sight, Seyd looked back in amazed terror, for at once he knew that this was no mere mortal beauty, but a miraculous and elemental loveliness such as it is given only to the inspired and the saintly to behold.

"Who art thou?" he asked in great fear, his flesh shaking as though it would fall asunder and dissolve.

"Ask not my name Seyd. Be content that I have been sent to thee in answer to thy unuttered prayers. Allah, in His great mercy, has understood that for thee and such as thee no mortal woman can suffice. But as it is necessary that the soul of woman

35

should unite with that even of the most learned and pious of mankind, such as I have been raised up to attend them in order that the miracle of nature's unity may be made complete."

Seyd was silent for a long time. "Much of what you say is dark to me," he said at last. "It may be that in my dreams and even while in prayer I have sought the perfect woman, though I knew it not. But how am I to know whether you are of the divine or a demon from Eblis? Sheitan sends strange and beautiful shapes to decoy the holy from their allegiance to The One."

The woman laughed. "Nay, seek not to number me among the devils," she said, "for were I a demon I might not utter the name of Allah. Nor might I enter this holy mosque, deserted as it is. And that I am more than woman, you have but to look at me to be convinced. Come, Seyd, reject me not, for it is the will of Allah that you should love and cherish me, of Allah who would have nothing created single, who has sent love into the world for all men's worship and acceptance."

As she spoke, she drew near, and, holding out her arms, folded him in an embrace so full of warm life and rapture, that, intoxicated, he returned it with almost equal ardour. His senses reeled at her kisses, his mood of cold insensibility fell from him like a garment outworn. For the first time he experienced the overwhelming miracle of love. The hours passed with dream-like rapidity in the little mosque. Seyd, the passionless, the chilly hearted, felt himself transported as if to the seventh heaven of delight. Profound as had been the rapture of his prayers, of what he called communion with Allah, this was an experience more divine.

"You have not told me your name," he said, "but already I know it. For you are Mystery, whom all men love, but whose love few achieve while still in life."

"Mystery I am, as thou sayest, O Seyd," she replied. "Yet is that not all of me. I am something more, something you encounter every day, something you love well, and for which you would gladly give your life, yet which daily you tread under your feet."

"You are also Love, mayhap?"

"Yes, Love I am, Love the most profound, a love surpassing that of the mother for the son, the sailor for the sea."

A thin light broke through the canopy of the darkness.

"It is the hour before dawn," whispered the woman, "we must part, Seyd my beloved. But come again to me soon. I shall keep tryst here each nightfall in the hope of meeting thee."

And so they parted with a lingering kiss. Seyd quickly made his way back to the barge to find that his four oarsmen had long fallen asleep. Awaking them, he was rowed speedily home. All night he dreamed of the woman he had met in the ruined mosque.

When he rose next day, it was to be assailed with doubt. Surely she must be a thing of evil, a ghoul such as the peasants spoke of; haunting ruined mosques and graveyards, a lamia such as the old legends told of, seeking to lure men to destruction. Yet of evil in her he had seen not the least admixture. Her bearing, her speech were natural and unaffected. It was chiefly the comprehension of something elemental in her, some power indescribable, that nurtured his misgivings.

All that day he walked in his garden, deep in meditation. That his lady could enter a mosque showed at least that she was not a thing, an appearance, sent by the powers of Eblis for his destruction. Holy mullahs and dervishes praying in the desert had been beset by such, and through their influence delivered over to the father of night. There was, of course, no imaginable test by which he could know absolutely that she was veritably a woman, unless he traced her to her dwelling-place. He recalled it as strange that when he had glanced back at the mosque when half-way to his barge that he had not seen her emerge from the only doorway the shrine had.

At nightfall, after a troubled day, he ordered his caique once more, and was rowed to the little jetty. It was now almost quite dark, and as he entered the mosque, he saw a white shape bending to and fro in the actions of the Moslem prayer. This dissolved his last fear that he had to deal with a creature unhallowed. Springing forward, he seized her in his arms, and was greeted with rapture.

"The day has been long," he said, "but its sorrows are over. I have thought of you through all the hours. I must know who you are—know your name."

"My name, beloved? Call me the Rose of Istanbul if thou wilt, for indeed I have none other you may know."

"The Rose of Istanbul! Truly that is a fair name enough, sweet, and so I shall call you, for the present at least. But when you become my bride, then I must know your true name."

"Your bride, Seyd? Am I not already your bride? Think you that the muttering of a few words by the Imam alone makes a man and woman one?"

"But I am resolved that you shall dwell in my house, moon of my eyes," cried Seyd in indignation. "Nay, it must be so."

"Let us forget the thoughts of men for the present," she replied, clinging to him. "Let us remember only the elemental things—the things which make up real existence."

And so the night passed as that before it had done, and night after night Seyd met the Rose of Istanbul. He could not put aside his longing that they should share existence wholly, by day as well as by night. He ached to see her in his house, to eat with her, to share the common things of life with her, and often did he tell her so. But to his pleadings she was silent. When he spoke thus, not a word did she answer.

At length he resolved to discover her identity, to find out where she lived. He had never, so far, seen her come or go at their rendezvous. So one night after leaving her in the little mosque as usual, he waited in the shadow of the trees which surrounded it, intent on following her.

Nearly half an hour passed, and he had almost resolved to retrace his steps to see whether she still remained in the mosque, when she passed the spot where he had concealed himself. Creeping stealthily from his hiding-place, he followed her. She walked slowly for some considerable distance over the rough bent which stretched between the seashore and the city. Suddenly the first ray of daylight stroked the sapphire dusk of night. Distracted from his intention for an instant by the beauty of the sight, an arrow of silver flying across an azure shadow, he cast his glance upward, and when he brough it back to the point where she had last appeared it was to find no trace of her. She had vanished as completely as though she had dissolved into the vapours of the morning which now began to rise from the plains behind the sea.

In a frenzy he ran onward, calling her name. "Rose, Rose of Istanbul, where are you?" But nothing could he see except the level waste where sand lay at the roots of each tuft of coarse grass, nothing could he hear except the low wind of sunrise sighing across the waste.

Despondently, he returned to his barge, and was rowed homeward. He had become aware that Zara, his chief wife, was suspicious of his nightly movements. Although she made no complaint, she frequently looked at him with deep reproach. As for the others, for days at a time he scarcely saw them. All three had become repugnant to him. To free himself from them was impossible.

Then he recalled that this woman who had taken him body and soul had told him that she was more than a woman, that she was, indeed, the answer to his prayer—a prayer he had been unconscious of offering up. Of what folly had he not been capable? That, good or evil, the Rose of Istanbul was a creature of spiritual mould he was now assured. Her disappearances on the seashore in the twinkling of an eye proved as much. He must see her no more, he must content himself with life as he found it; as a true man should.

So no more he went to the mosque in the little wood. Days passed, and, although grief gnawed at his heart as a serpent, he kept to his own house at nights. His wife Zara was pleased with him, and even refrained from tormenting the little Greek, Danäe, while the young but experienced Ayesha, who had been married before to an elderly roué, smiled secretly and tittered when he went to the casement, opening it on the view of the Golden Horn.

But he could not harden his heart against the Rose of Istanbul, for the lure of her was such as it is not given to man to resist, the lure of earth, of air, of nature, of the deep, indwelling life which lies in the soil's womb, in the bodies of trees, in the breath of life which we call the wind. All that the eye might see, all that the ear might hear, recalled the miracle of her, who was compounded of atoms and essences natural and delectable. The woods were her hair, the planets her eyes, the sea her spirit. And Seyd knew that she might not be escaped by any man, because as she had said, she was not only woman, but all that woman in her essential native vigour and power and divine sweetness brings to man in one body—the rapturous spirit of that earth of which he is himself a part, the less vivid, the less dædal part, the nymphic fire that from the oak conceives the dryad, that from the stream brings forth the naiad, that pagan fury which not only receives the life of which man is the vessel, but which has power, like his mother the earth, to bring it to harvest and fruition.

Stunned for a space by the revelation of what he had lost, he leaped from his divan with the frenzy of a man who had cast away a whole world. His slaves shrank from him in terror when they beheld him. With speechless gestures, he commanded them to prepare the caique. They obeyed, and in a few moments he was cleaving the waters of the Golden Horn once more, the foam rising upon the prow, turning into snow the reflected heaven of Bosphorous.

And so he came to the little mosque and found her there. Once more he was enfolded in her arms, he drank of her loveliness.

"Ah," she cried, gazing into his eyes with rapture, "all is well at last. You know, Seyd, you understand. For I am what comes to all poets, I am the soil as woman, as bride, she who at last arises out of the earth they love better than themselves to cherish them and be with them always. I am the Rose of Istanbul!"

*   *   *

The Imam's tale was finished; and the man from Ankara, who had been showing signs of impatience, rose to regale us with a tale of what can happen when people follow wills o' the wisp, perhaps as a contrast to the ethereal in Seyd's story . . .

This is what he said.

HIDING IN A HUSBAND'S BEARD

Zara peered through the lattices at the swarming hurry of the broad lane, a stream of vivid and noisy life. How attractive it was down there, how magnetic was the nearness of humanity! Stanbul was a city electrified by a new existence since Kamal Pasha had chased the past out of its crooked highways and had, by ukase and precept, compelled people to the life of the modern world, unveiling the women, banishing the fez, bundling all the rubbish out of the attic of the centuries. But for Zara there might be no fourth and feverish decade of an awakened twentieth century. Her patriarchal spouse remained one of Turkey's 'untouchables', he would not conform to the new social attitudes, even the least of the sumptuary laws concerning head and footwear was anathema to his conservatism. In a word, he was among the last monuments of a Turkey which had squatted on its carpet, sucked at its hookah, and shut up its womenkind like pigeons in a loft.

Forty years in advance of him in respect of youth, Zara loathed him from beard to turned-up shoes. The new age had dawned while she was still learning French and picking out her scales upon the piano. And before she was yet sixteen, Selim had doddered into her life with his accursed splay beard like an osprey's nest, his long, dolorous cheeks and his money, the money which had weighed down the faltering balance of her father's will. He was no more to be escaped than the earth one walks upon or the air one breathes. He was man, he was marriage, he was the abomination of choiceless matrimony which so many Turkish women in the past have dreaded while they accepted it. He was prison, he was old age, he was death.

And so, when women's quarters were being swept from the face of Turkey, when veils were being rent and the liberty of high heels attained, Zara was still the inmate of a harem—a harem of one, it is true, yet a jail none the less, from the traceried casements of which it was possible to see laughing girls taking their freedom on the pavements outside while she must amuse herself like an odalisque with her French novels, her monkey and her piano. Every laugh which reached her from below was an insult, every snatch of song a challenge. The world had begun all over again, the liberty of thousands had been achieved, only she was a prisoner, the creature of a custom-deluded patriarch.

Zara glanced out of the window again. Two smartly dressed girls passed on the arms of their cavaliers, laughing and flirting. To one-and-twenty it was intolerable. With a cry of fury, she dashed the yellowback novel to the floor. Selim had gone to Ankara. He would be absent for many days. When would she have such a chance again? Yes, it was a day to let everything go, to take any risk. She rang the bell on the little table beside her with rather unnecessary violence.

Black Qulsa appeared, running, her ivories well revealed, as usual. "Yes, yes," she cried. "Coffee, effen', coffee, effen'?"

"Drink your own coffee," said Zara gaily. "I am going for a drive."

"In the old carriage, yes," cried Qulsa, clapping her hands. "And I will go with the effen'."

Driving was the one privilege Selim permitted, but the excursion must always be made in the ancient family *shandrydan* and in the company of Qulsa.

"The Angel of Confusion seize the old carriage," hissed Zara, "and you also, Qulsa. You must stay at home. I mean to pay some calls and will take a motor-car. Run to the nearest garage and have one sent round at once!"

"But the master, effen', he does not like motor-cars," wailed Qulsa, "Motor-cars are the chariots of Sheitan."

"The master effen' is in Ankara," Zara said flatly, "and you will obey my commands. I wish to know how it feels to ride in a motor-car, Sheitan or no Sheitan."

Qulsa put as good a face as she could upon the matter and ran off to order the car. Zara drew from her wardrobe the amazing frock of dark Chinese silk which she wore when she paid calls to other ladies, and the Parisian hat she sported on such rare occasions, and proceeded to make her toilet, humming a little song of release and freedom. In a quarter of an hour the car was at the door. She kept it waiting for scarcely two minutes.

"A man drives the car," muttered Qulsa as sententiously as though she were a living copy-book duenna, "and that is evil."

"Did you expect Sheitan to drive it, fool?" laughed Zara, "or I suppose you think he is hidden in the engine. I will be back in a few hours."

"Where to, madame?" asked the chauffeur with an obsequious smile.

"The Hotel Paradise," whispered Zara, not wishing Qulsa to hear, and jumped in lightly.

The streets were gay with the afternoon sun of that old Istanbul which in her modern disguise and frontage looked almost new, as if saying in her masquerade of up-to-date cafés, tweed suits, Parisian frocks and coiffures, taxis, streamlined cars and buses, "I maintain my Turkish soul but give consent to an unwritten treaty that I will go European outwardly at least." Kamal had retained Istanbul for the Turks and had modernized them and it by a single *coup*. As they raced now through the narrow streets, and now through broad boulevards Zara felt her blood racing in rhythm with the throbbing of the engine. If this swift passage was the prelude to *la vie moderne* she was never going back to the old barbarous stuffiness of the sexist prison she occupied with a negress and a monkey. The car stopped gently. So this was the Hotel Paradise of which her emancipated friends had told her so often? Without a qualm she descended, tipped the chauffeur with a lavishness which badly shook his faith in the professional adage that women were greed incarnate, and fluttered through the revolving doors into the crowded lounge.

Women are the true heroines of occasion. Even the bold, bad Byron felt awkward in society after a couple of years' well-deserved banishment, but this little uncaged Zara flaunted it clean through the labyrinth of the tables to the *thé-dansant* behind, and sitting down in a vacant corner, ordered tea as coolly as if she were its oldest *habitué*. The orchestra was playing one of the bounding, pulsating things she had heard on her gramophone and which she recognized at once as the Havana. How she had practised the rhythm all by herself from instructions given in the friendly pages of "Femina". *La vie heureuse!* That was the phrase in her mind. But now, a partner;

where was he to be found? She recognized quite a number of girl acquaintances scattered about the room, but one and all, they were accompanied by male escorts. To approach any in the circumstances was impossible. But how they stared at her, the flown bird, the manumitted odalisque. She choked down the feeling of dread as the long patriarchal visage of Selim hovered among the exhaled smoke of the cigarette she had just lit. Ankara was in Asia Minor. This was Europe, and the waters of the Straits continued to roll between. For her they would roll for ever, for she was determined that she never would go back to that osprey's nest beard and the red-and-gold cushions, come what may.

Selim's beard had scarcely vanished when the desired dancing-partner stood before her, tall, courtly, solicitous. In another moment she was in his arms, swaying across the glassy floor to the staccato rhythm of the Havana, as though she had danced it a hundred times. At least this was life, freedom, the full surge of existence. The dark vivid appeal of the eyes which looked down into hers made her heart beat wildly. This was indeed a prince of romance, handsome as a hero of legend. The almost flawless tan of the face with its small moustache and rather full lips, the faultlessly tailored body, inspired her with a sense of perfect fulfilment. This was, indeed, the inevitable man for whom she had been waiting since first she had dreamed of love as apart from the undesirable theme of conventional marriage.

The music ceased and they sat down and talked as though they were old friends. Their converse seemed at once to flow into channels of mutual interest. He was tender, chivalrous—so chivalrous. Beside him, the thought of Selim was like death compared with life. They danced again, talked still more. He gently insisted upon a glass of sherry, then another glass. The unusual liquor sent a golden fire through her blood, she found herself confiding everything. Gently he understood, he bowed his dark head, he agreed with her that life as she had experienced it was unthinkable. It was an unthinkable thing that she should go back to this ancient ogre of a husband. She must trust him, must leave everything to him. Would she do so? She would. Then he would meet Selim, would arrange for a separation. All would be well. Meanwhile he would take her to a place where she would have every liberty and comfort until these annoying proceedings were over. They hammered out the pros and cons of it, and in a couple of hours had mapped out her life for more than as many years.

He glanced at his watch.

"My car is outside," he said with a dazzling smile. "Shall we go?"

She nodded. Was he not a prince, could he not be trusted? A man with such eyes, with such a smile, whom she felt she had known all her life. They rose, and made their way through the lounge. He left her to bring up his car. It rolled up, glittering, luxurious. He tucked her into the front seat beside him, and the Paradise Hotel slipped quickly behind them.

She must have been in the Paradise for hours. How the time had passed. It was early night, and the streets were ablaze and magical as she could not have dreamed they would be. How amazing was the outside world. As if on the wings of sorcery they left the city behind, and rolled swiftly northward, to where she did not know. The flat night-bound land lay on one side, on the other the dark cobalt of the Bosphorus, sprinkled with reflected stars. Now and again they flashed past low white houses, huts, isolated clumps of poplar or cypress. Almost for the first time she saw the world apart from house or causeway. How strange and enticing it seemed, an unburdened plane of freedom. How silent her handsome tanned friend had grown.

Lights showed dimly through the darkness, and the car came to a halt. He descended. He helped her to alight. They stood before a long, low building with a balcony in front, a house whose windows gleamed and from which came the sound of wilder music than she had heard at the Paradise.

They entered, to a scene of wild abandon. This was the modern Turkish version of the American roadhouse, the new Istanbul's notion of how they did things on the outskirts of the whirling cities of the wicked West. Only it still held a suspicion of the more simply audacious East. On a small stage danced a quartette of ladies of that type of Russian refugee which seems to dominate the half-world in the city of Constantine. Scenery would have been a work of supererogation, for mere oilpaint could never have vied with the profligate pigmentation of the dancers, which shamed the glow of the Chinese lanterns swinging above them. The trumpets of the small band blared, and glasses clinked ostentatiously.

For a moment Zara faltered. The Paradise had been polite, conventional, but this! And was this her princely escort, this man with the demon's face, who called loudly for arrak and hailed the sodden habitués of the place by nickname! The bedizened, smoke-filled room with its fumes of raw liquor and its noisy racket spun round her. This . . . This was infamy, shame, the abomination of profligacy! Of such were the ditches which stank on the frontiers of romance, the open graves in which its dead corpses were flung. Her prince had become a dark mocking spirit holding a poisoned cup.

She turned to fly, where she did not know. Anything to escape this hell and hasten her to the house of Selim. But his hand was upon her wrist, and she strained uselessly towards the door. Suddenly the blaring music ceased with a jolt. One of the dancing female Russians had leapt from the stage, screaming like a fury in voluble French. With a bound she was upon the 'Prince', nor did any seek to stop her. To have done so would have been to put an end to the species of furious interlude they relished even more than the fiery liquor they swilled.

Some ancient and deep-seated grudge it was that inspired the Russian lady's ample vocabulary to rise above its common limitations. A lengthy torrent of recrimination erupted stormily from between the carmined lips, a tale of betrayal, of the merchandise of a woman's soul. This harpy had once been confiding, innocent as Zara herself. The base audience applauded in the intervals between the desperate sentences of long pent-up rhetoric. This speech had evidently seethed in the woman's heart and brain for years. The 'Prince' stood statuesquely silent, a devil's leer peeping beneath the small dark moustache. Once he laughed aloud, and as he did so his grip on Zara's wrist tightened.

The Russian fumbled among her bosom's finery. A fat man in the foreground uttered a warning cry. In her hand she held a long, bead-encrusted phial. To her lips she carried it swiftly, none preventing her. Then, as swiftly, she dashed the contents in the face of the man before her.

For an instant the 'Prince' stood still as though incapable of motion. Then a thin greenness like that which gathers upon bronze, smeared the tan flesh, and with a shriek such as only a sudden quenching of the sight can extort, he fell writhing to the floor. Babel ensued, the yelling of Sheol. Clapping her hands upon her ears, Zara rushed from the place. There stood the car which had hurried her through the night to this infamy and disgrace.

A hand was upon her shoulder.

"Get in," commanded a voice, that of the Russian woman. "I will drive."

Feeling dull and stupified Zara obeyed. In a few minutes they had left the roadhouse a league behind. Then the Russian applied the brakes.

"You damned little fool," she hissed. "Couldn't you see? He's the world's worst! In a month you'd have been a wretched little slave in a house in Paris or Buenos. You'd have gone through the self-same hell as I had to endure—years of it. Yes, I kept the flask handy for him. I knew we'd meet some time. He'll never see a woman's face again. Where have you come from?"

Zara told her all in hurried stammers. The Russian nodded with a harsh pitying expression of perfect comprehension.

"I'll drive you right home," she said. "Beard or no beard, whether he's as old as Methuselah, stick to your husband," she counselled. "He's your pillar, your salvation, don't you see? For such as you, innocent that you are, the outside world is hell . . . worse than hell."

"What'll you do?" sobbed Zara as she floundered on the cushions in mounting hysteria.

"Me? I'll sell his car and get out," promptly answered the Russian. "It's Budapest for me. I'll take your cloak," she added coolly. "Experience is cheap that's paid for by a few yards of silk and ostrich trimming."

And Zara agreed—most wholeheartedly. To her the beard of Selim had become a bush in which to hide herself from the world.

*   *   *

When dawn came and the caravan started I had thought that the friendship and telling of tales would cease, with the hardships of the way and the separation of one man from another which was caused by the need for every one of us to look after his prayers, his goods, his beasts—but no.

Sometimes as we walked or rode side by side, one or another of us would relate a true narrative or remembered legend, a story first or second hand. Sometimes, as we went southwards to the Syrian border, we would stop for food or water, and one would regale others with a tale. As the weather grew warmer, we had to travel through the cool of the night. During our daytime rest stops, however, we hardly ever slept as well as in the night-time—and more and more stories started to appear.

The Egyptian, as we called him because he spoke with the accent of that country, recited this story to me as a true one, on one of those nights when we rode side by side through Turkey. He had studied medicine in Britain, and I recount the narrative in the very Western way in which he told it . . .

THE CASTLE OF THE CANNIBAL

Ever since the gangway had been lifted at Colombo, and I saw the sunburnt visage of a middle-aged Englishman under a particularly worn Solar helmet, I had thought that I knew the man. Constantly I had come face to face with him when the steamer ploughed its way through the sea towards Aden. Beyond a side-glance this curious and aloof man defied acquaintance. But something fascinated me about my fellow-passenger—he had an almost eerie influence on me. One night when the stars hung from the sky in bunches like giant and glowing pieces of the moon, that enchanting scene so gripped me that my coffee cup slipped from my hand; it rolled over the railing and fell in the lap of someone sitting in his deck chair. The sleeper woke up with a start, as if from a trance, and as I hastened to apologize, my eyes met the same mysterious man who, I thought, had been making an extra effort to avoid me.

After profound apologies, I resolved to take the opportunity. "Excuse me," I said, "but have we not met before?" The man looked up. "Yes!" he grunted, "yes, perhaps we have met on the moon." That grunt of his—a little mannerism as it was—flashed a host of memories. It emboldened me. "We have not met in the moon, old boy," I spoke half humorously. "Come, come, Charlie, do you forget that Pathology classroom?" He had stiffened slightly, then he gave it up, and the whole association of our undergraduate days returned.

He had failed twice in his finals, the professor had been hard on him, he thought. The War came on, he served in the Army, and then after a disastrous love affair, went to the East to lose himself. But now he was returning. He did not want to know any of his old haunts. Whether Muriel had gone to Canada or had married someone else he did not care. He just wanted to spend a quiet summer in England after a dreadful time in the wilds of Sri Lanka.

Not till the steward was putting out the lights did we realize that we were on the wrong side of the deck, where ladies slept. But Charles Munro, though this is not his real name for obvious reasons, besides being a good all-round cricketer, and a mimic of his national bard, was also a good story-teller. What he began to tell me of experiences in the back of beyond interested me so much that we went to the men's side of the deck. Within ten minutes we too had brought up our mattresses on the deck, and I was once again listening to him. "You did not stick long to your botanical researches?" I asked. "Well!" he said, with that Scottish drawl which was characteristic of him, "Well, you see, I sort of got into the man-eaters business." "Man-eaters! Good heavens! You were not amongst cannibals?" Yet what he related brought him as close to being a man-eater as any civilized man wishes to be. And it was as well for him that the spell was broken.

It transpired that he had qualified in some way or other in pharmacology in Kandy, and by way of research, he had sallied forth to collect some herbs, which the local people thought would cure malaria. One day he set out in search of those uncharted regions of the island which even the aircraft have not been able to penetrate. Charlie was desperate, he did not care what happened to him. He would be an explorer, a discoverer of herbs that would free mankind from fever. But now I must let him use his own words.

"Desperately," he said, "I wandered on, the terror of the jungle on me. It was unnerving and paralysing my volition. I was indeed lost in these endless and pitiless leagues of enveloping greenness without hope of exit or rescue. Fool that I had been not to take the advice of my *shikari* guide! I did not know Ceylon, I had not bargained for such conditions as I now found myself in. Beaten, exhausted, I floundered on mechanically, my rifle feeling as heavy as the beam of a house on my tired shoulders.

"Suddenly I heard the baying of a hound in the distance. The noise, menacing as it was, aroused my flickering hopes. It would, if followed up, lead me out of the labyrinth. Again the deep baying sounded on the calm evening air, then, as if the whole of Hades had broken loose, it was succeeded by a chorus of such infernal barking and yelling as I had never heard before. The furious din checked my progress, I halted and listened.

50

Would it be safe to go in that direction? It would certainly not be safe to stay where I was, and the hubbub, threatening as it sounded, would at least lead me out of my perilous position—to land me in a worse one, perhaps. Well, I had come to the end of my tether and had no choice. I decided to face the music, and pressed on in the direction of what seemed to be a pack of hounds let loose and hot on the track of their prey.

"Then, suddenly, I stopped dead once more, for the awful thought had occurred to me that I myself might be the prey, the object of that clamorous quest. Even as I halted, I noticed that the jungle had grown less dense. Pressing forward, I emerged all at once into the bright sunshine and in view of a strange picture.

"In a clearing between jungle and jungle, an island of plain between two seas of forest, stood the most incongruous building it has ever been my lot to see—yes, truly, for this is not fiction, but absolute fact. Think of a mediæval tower cast out of England or Normandy into the midst of a Cingalese landscape! On one side of it stood a long low building, evidently kennels, and issuing from this I saw a pack of some twenty large hounds of a breed I was quite unable to place. No two of them were alike, and I judged them to be mongrels between the bloodhound and other large breeds; at least many of them had undoubted bloodhound characteristics. I have seen such dogs in the Portuguese towns of India, and I believe they had been brought from Pondicherry.

"Behind them stood a curious figure, a Western man in striped pyjamas, the trousers of which were tucked into long, laced-up field-boots. He wore a sun helmet, and at that distance I could not see his face. But I was not occupied at the moment with personal idiosyncrasies or appearances. The hounds, sighting me, gave full cry, and came at me like a speckled wave.

"'Look out,' I yelled, raising my rifle, 'If your dogs attack me, I shall shoot—and it won't be at the dogs.'

"Their master heard, even at that distance, and snapped out an order. Instantly the brutes came to a stop, whimpering and whining like a pack of disappointed wolves. I walked slowly towards the man with the solar helmet, and now I could see his eyes—curious eyes they were, eager, strained and bloodshot, the restless ones of a debauchee, it seemed to me.

" 'It's late for hunting,' I said, 'but your hounds have got me out of a fix. I was lost in the jungle.'

" 'Several people have been lost there,' he replied in strange but cultivated tones, although with a strong foreign accent. 'That's why I bring the dogs out. They have rescued not a few wanderers.'

" 'That's an odd house of yours, if you'll excuse me for saying so.' I ventured. 'Quite like the ogre's castle in a fairy tale, isn't it?''

" '*Ogre's* castle,' he repeated. 'You think so? Well, you're all in, I expect. You had better come inside and lie down for a bit,' and turning and whistling to his dogs he led the way to the tower. Within, it was comfortable enough, clearly for tropical conditions. The ground floor was the living-room, two airy bedrooms composed the second storey. As to the third, I only saw it once.

"I learned that my host's name was Kreimer, or so I shall style him. He was a heavy, cumbrous-looking man of obviously lazy habits, about fifty perhaps, fleshy and unwholesome. His only servant was a Cingalese, a creature of quite extraordinary suavity.

"But I was in no case to quarrel with circumstances, and after an excellent supper of curry which might have been cooked in the Club at Calcutta, I was shown to my room and slept like a man in a legend. And while I slept I dreamed—nor were my dreams pleasant.

"They were chaotic and indescribable, those dreams of mine, but their central motif seemed to be a horrible unnerving sensation of constant rustling, to which the baying of the hounds played a menacing accompaniment. Rustle, rustle, the weird sound continued throughout the night, like the leaves of a windswept wood in June, and, even though I slept, I had a sensation of the nearness of disembodied presences which filled me with a vague unrest. I awoke unrefreshed and almost as weary as I had been the night before, but I washed and dressed, and descending, put the best face on things I could. Kreimer was in the living-room, and what I saw him do I did not like.

"At first I thought he was drinking a glass of wine. But when I drew closer, I saw to my horror that it was not wine.

" 'Good morning,' he said affably enough, as he finished his drink. 'You seem surprised at the nature of my refreshment, but it's doctor's orders.'

" 'Indeed,' I said most inadequately, wishing myself for some instinctive reason a thousand miles away from this man.

" 'Yes, I find fresh blood wonderful as a morning pick-me-up,' he continued almost carelessly. 'Ever tried it?'

" 'Good gracious, no!' I retorted, suddenly angry, I knew not why.

" 'But you drink milk, don't you?" he asked, as if surprised, 'and what is milk but white blood?'

"I made no reply, and we sat down to a breakfast of kedgeree and coffee, well served by his Cingalese. How it was I came to accept his invitation to stay for a week I cannot say. The man had a strange fascination about him, and I have always been strongly attracted by odd personalities.

" 'This is a wonderful spot for cheetah,' he said, as he lit a cheroot. 'I course them with the hounds. Suppose we try our luck before tiffin? You won't need a gun, it's all dog-work. Better start at once while it's reasonably cool, if you don't mind.'

"He had touched me on one of my weak spots. Of course cheetah are not usually hunted that way at all, but I was keen to see a new method. So in ten minutes he had routed out the dogs, and was waiting for me at the door.

" 'By the way,' he said, looking at me strangely, 'the dogs aren't used to you. and they're a trifle uncertain with strangers. Suppose you walk towards the jungle and watch the proceedings from cover. My man and I will drive them in the opposite direction, and as it's all flat country hereabouts you'll get a capital view of the sport when we rouse one of the spotted fellows. What do you say?'

"I looked at the hounds, leaping, snapping and snarling, and he didn't have to ask me twice. So, while he and his man held them on the leash, I made for the wall of trees about a quarter of a mile away.

"I had gone, perhaps, a couple of hundred yards when I heard the yapping and whining change suddenly to the noise of a pack in full cry. Surprised that they had already roused the cheetah, I turned. The pack, with baying heads and tails high in air was rushing straight in my direction!

"For an instant I stood stock-still, unable to believe that I was their quarry. But a second glance sufficed to make it certain. The brutes were running towards me as if possessed, and Kreimer was waving them on with halloos and hunting cries as a man might a pack of beagles. With a sudden oath of terrified anger, I put down my head and dashed in the direction of the jungle at top speed.

"Well for me was it that I was a sprinter in those days, and in good form. One stumble, one false step, and I should have been done for. I had more than two hundred yards to make, and the brutes were not more than half that distance behind me when my warning came. I ran like a man who feels death clutching at his windpipe, sobbing, cursing, in a surge of frightful anger, My heart rose in my throat and half smothered me like the grip of an enemy. By the time I made the sheltering trees I was all in, merely reduced to a crumpled pair of lungs, drawing like a broken bellows. With the last of my frenzied strength I shinned up a tree and stared down at the howling brindled demons below me, leaping and frothing like maddened wolves. In another two minutes Kreimer had come up.

" 'A thousand apologies, my dear young man', he shouted, 'the brutes got out of hand. I simply couldn't hold them.'

" 'You devil,' I sobbed, 'didn't I see you driving them on, you infernal murderer!'

" 'You're mistaken, I assure you,' he said suavely, looking at me strangely, almost hungrily, none the less. 'I was shouting at them to keep them back.'

" 'Tell your man to take them to the kennels,' I said, 'for I have something to say to you.'

" 'Certainly, he'll take them back,' he replied with a great show of willingness, and gave the necessary orders. At a word the hounds, which seemed to be absolutely under the control of the Cingalese, trotted away behind him to the kennels. When they were at a reasonable distance I descended and faced Kreimer. But I faced a man with a revolver in his hand.

"He might have bristled with revolvers, but I was instantly at his throat. Then a strange thing happened. As I seized him, he crumpled up like paper in my arms, and slipped to the ground. I fell heavily on top of him. His white face stared into mine. I knew he was dead as I looked into the glazed eyes.

"The heart had given way suddenly like a broken piston. Horrified and shaken, I called loudly to the Cingalese. At the third cry he came running to me. He bent over the face of the dead.

" 'This is no marval,' he said calmly. 'He was a bad man. The gods have slain him out of the sky. Maybe, some demon of the forest . . .' and he looked at me fearfully.

" 'Help me to carry him to the house,' I said, and without another word we bore the body back to that strange tower which it had so lately inhabited.

" 'Yes, he was a bad man,' babbled the Cingalese sententiously. 'He hunted other men . . .'

" 'What are you telling me?' I gasped, overcome with horror. 'Do you mean to say the man was a madman?'

" 'No,' he replied gravely. 'He made me his slave and I had to obey. Strangers lost in the jungle came here, he hunted them with his hounds, and then . . .'

" 'And then what?' I asked, but received no reply.

"The thing seemed incredible. Entering the house, I went through Kreimer's papers. The man was Russian, a land-owner, from the Crimea. His diary showed that he had undergone the experience of a terrible famine. Perhaps that had . . . but such surmises are better left unwritten.

"I resolved to remain in the Castle until such time as some official came our way. Someone from the Woods and Forests Department would surely pay us a visit before long, I felt assured. I had nothing to fear. Kreimer had attempted my life and his death was due entirely to mishap, for I had scarce touched him. My conscience was clear. And, moreover, it was impossible to communicate with the authorities from that jungle-surrounded place.

"We buried Kreimer that evening in the compound, and I made up my mind to shoot every one of the hounds next morning. That night I slept not at all. I was consious of the same rustling in my bedroom, a weird sound as of bodiless things moving in the darkness, so I rose and lit the lamp and smoked and read until dawn, when I fell at last into an uneasy dozing.

"And now comes the most dreadful part of my tale. How it

55

happened, I do not presume to be able to say, but, after a few days, I had no inclination to quit Cain Castle, as I came to call the strange tower in which I found myself. At first it was something resembling curiosity which detained me there, that and a resolve to await the coming of someone in authority to whom I could relate the truth of what had happened to Kreimer. But, after a few days, I began to feel with growing horror and dismay that I was becoming attached to the place, that, indeed, it held a weird kind of fascination for me. I grew tolerant even of the hounds, and felt more than disinclined to destroy them. After all . . .

"It was on the fourth day, I believe, that I began to experience a new phase of this peculiar obsession, for that is the only word I can discover for it. The horror with which I regarded the place and everything connected with it had entirely disappeared, and I found that not only could I tolerate Cain Castle, but that I even had a relish for the tower and its surroundings. No longer did I dread the rustling noises in the darkness of the night. I felt, on the other hand, something almost companionable and friendly in it.

"My conscience seemed numbed and clouded. I began to feel as though my very personality were undergoing an alteration. I remember now with horror the ghastly change which crept over me in that accursed place, but at the time, if you will believe me, I experienced nothing of the nausea with which I now regard the unnatural metamorphosis which I saw gradually creeping over me, the new and vile character which invaded and enveloped my ego like a demoniac possession.

"It is difficult for you to realize the nature of the strange and occult influences native to that environment. Little by little the influence, the horror, grew upon me. Soon I was as a child in its grasp. I walked about like a man in a trance. The Cingalese saw the change and spoke warning words full of enigmatical meaning. He might as well have spoken to the wall around us. Some dark power immeasurably mightier than man had me in its grasp, soul and body. The baying of the hounds had become as music to me, and curiously enough, they now displayed no unfriendliness, but leapt with joy at their fences when I appeared, fawning on me and licking my hands.

"One cloudy morning, dark, hot, mercilessly tropical, with

the threat of thunder in the air, I rose, duller than ever in mind, and conscious of a craving which I could not describe to myself, a horrible physical craving, a wild hunger which was yet not of the nature of ordinary hunger, for the excellent breakfast the Cingalese placed before me remained untasted, arousing only nausea. Like a beast I stalked about the house, mooning from window to window. Ha, what was that! The hounds were baying wildly. Something within me, something unspeakably wild and savage, leapt tigerishly at the sound. I looked toward the jungle. A man in a white drill suit was staggering out of it, evidently in the same predicament as that in which I had found myself some ten days before. Then he seemed to disappear.

"I rushed upstairs to the top storey of the tower, the better to get a sight of him and his movements, springing up the crazy stone steps like a panther. A wild blood-lust possessed me, I experienced the overpowering joy and triumph that the greater beasts must feel at sight of their prey.

"Behind me the Cingalese cried and babbled.

" 'Sir, sir, go not up there,' he pleaded. 'There is something there . . . something unholy.'

"The upper storey of the tower consisted of two rooms. So far I had only entered that on the opposite side, a room full of books, guns and hunting tackle. That which looked toward the jungle was locked. Now, in a frenzy of passion, I threw myself upon it. The crazy lock parted, and I was propelled into the place with terrific force. Stumbling to the cobwebbed window, I gazed through it with distended eyes, panting like a tiger behind bars. Ah, now I caught sight of the little white figure once again!

"Then revulsion, horror, loathing, descended on me like a quenching flood, burning out the fires of the abominable ardour I had felt. I knelt beside that grim relic, my face buried in my hands, quivering with shame and self-aversion, a spirit newly escaped from some awful pit and limbo of ancient devilry in which I had languished for days of half-realized abandonment. What had I nearly become? With a cry I gazed around me. The room was literally stacked with human bones, the horrid trophies which Kreimer, the man-demon, the cannibal, had garnered there as mementoes of his unspeakable orgies.

"Nearly beside myself, I rushed below, through the compound and towards the now recumbent figure at the verge of the jungle. I had scarcely run more quickly when pursued by the hell-hounds on the day of the unspeakable Kreimer's death. The Cingalese followed me. We raised the fallen form, but it was lifeless.

"Two days later I was myself on the road to civilization, accompanied by the Cingalese. But before I went, I loaded every rifle and revolver in the tower—and then I entered the kennels and did what I had to do there quickly and mercifully. When the last of the demon-dogs had yelped out its life, I turned to the tower. The Cingalese and I gathered all the dry timber on which we could lay hands, and heaping it in the lower storey, I set it alight. In a couple of hours nothing remained of the Castle but the blackened walls.

"When I returned to Colombo, I set inquiries afoot, and revealed the outline of the history of the place. It had been built by an eccentric Englishman of means in the early part of the nineteenth century, an astrologer, who had retired to that remote district so that he might the better devote himself to the study of his mysterious art free from disturbance or interference. For at least a generation it had lain vacant and practically ruined, until, some five years before the opening of my story, it had been found and renovated by Kreimer. The mysterious disappearance of explorers in such a country did not arouse any especial remark, as it was thought they had perished in the neighbouring jungle, which possessed a particularly bad reputation as a wilderness easy to lose oneself in. At the same time it seems peculiar that the very considerable number of people who had gone amissing in that particular locality during Kreimer's tenancy of the accursed tower had not aroused suspicion."

When Charlie finished, I felt that I could not sleep. The very waves of the ocean seemed to be full of yelping, barking dogs. But he was asleep in no time. He needed it more.

*   *   *

What the consensus of the caravan would have been as to the truth of this tale I had no idea, and I did not therefore speak of it to the others when we camped. Far more typical of traditional stories, yet with a haunting undertone of "something else" was the offering which came, soon afterwards, from the Bard from Azarbaijan, a member of a long line of story-tellers, who regaled us with it as we were leaving Turkish soil.

THE PRINCESS WHO WAS A PRINCE

"May thy grandsires burn alive!" swore the Shah at his Grand Vizier; "you so far forgot yourself as to defeat me in the game of chess!" He foamed at the mouth as he continued: "And I am your own master, King of Kings!"

The Vizier hung his head in shame.

And the King of Kings, who sat on the throne of Persia, wanted to punish the Grand Vizier; yet even in those days, a monarch had to find a better excuse to chop off his minister's head than a mere defeat in a chess game.

"Ah!" he remembered, "tell me, why have you not reminded the Sultan of Azerbaijan about complying with our demands?" Here was clearly a case of neglect in the performance of his official's duty. Indirectly, the Grand Vizier had to pay for his attitude at the chess table.

But the Sultan of Azerbaijan was in a quandary. He had seven daughters, but every one of them was more ugly than the other. The Princess Peri had ears like miniature fans; the Princess Kulsum, because of her corpulence, had gained the sobriquet of "Sultan's Little Elephant"; the Princess Banu was a dwarf—and so on, each having her peculiar deformity. To present any of these to the Shah of Shahs, one of the most famous connoisseurs of female beauty, was simply to court immediate invasion, and the conclusion of the royal house of Azerbaijan.

So the Sultan bewailed his deficiency in daughters. "Lo!" he cried, "here have I seven useless wenches on my hands who do nothing but quarrel and stuff themselves with sickly sweets, *rahat loukum* from morning to night, and when danger threatens me and the gift of one or other would avert it, none of them is of any avail! Surely Allah has afflicted me for some secret sin that I know not of."

And in his agony he sought the advice of his only son, the Prince Musa. Now Musa was the son of a Circassian woman whom the Sultan had loved very much, and whom he had elevated to the rank of his principal wife. And Prince Musa was by the far the handsomest young man in Azerbaijan. On the day he was called into counsel with his father, he was just seventeen, and like the sun to look upon, with his bright golden curls, Greek nose and Cupid's mouth. But he was also one of the most warlike princes in Islam, and already had proved himself a valiant fighter in the wars with the Franks. His lithe, girlish shape held more strength and activity than that of many a seeming Hercules, and in native subtlety and cunning not the wisest doctors and imams could match him.

He joined his father in the summer pavilion in the midst of the lake, a palace of glass where the old man was wont to amuse himself at chess with the Vizier. The Sultan was a bad chess player, but the Vizier was a worse, and that was why he liked to play chess with him. And when the Prince arrived the Sultan had just given check to the Vizier's king.

"Alas!" he cried, "that so easily I may give check to this piece of ivory which bears the name of king, and that I cannot with equal simplicity give pause to this tyrant of Persia. For what did Allah give me wit if not to defend mine own possessions?"

"Be not troubled, my father," said Prince Musa softly, for his voice was like a young girl's. "Young as I am, I believe I have solved the difficulty which causes you such vexation."

"My son," replied the Sultan hopefully, "you are young indeed, but well am I aware that few either in the east or the west possess your ready wit and excellent good sense. Come, then, reveal to us the manner in which we can placate this Shah who wants a wife from every land from Cathay to Africa."

"Being a man and a soldier," said Prince Musa, "I do not use a mirror. Yet I have caught sight of myself in my mother's looking-glass, and know that it has pleased Allah the Merciful to give me the lineaments of a fair young woman. I propose, your Majesty, that you send me to the Shah of Persia as your handsomest daughter."

"What?" bellowed the Sultan, "are you in your senses? I have heard and read that great mental brilliance frequently verges on madness, but I did not suspect such gifts as yours of imbecile admixture. You speak folly, my son."

"Not so fast, your Majesty," droned the Vizier, "for I think I can see much wisdom in the suggestion. Let us hear the Prince to the end."

"My father," said Musa, "what is your chief objection to the scheme, if I may ask as much?"

Now the Sultan was flustered. "In the name of the demon Eblis," he shouted, "did any man ever put such a question to another? But since you are so lacking in acumen, let me take you further. You betake yourself to the Shah in the guise of a bride. The nuptials are duly celebrated, the bridal chamber is reached . . ."

At this point the Prince was seized with uncontrollable laughter. Peal upon peal resounded through the pavilion. The Vizier at last joined in it, but Sultan grew red and still redder, and in his annoyance upset the chessboard.

"Sire," said the Prince at last, when he could speak coherently, "pardon me, I beg of you, but surely you cannot but believe that such a contingency must have occurred to me."

"And how do you propose to circumvent it?" demanded the Sultan angrily.

"That, sire, you must leave to me," replied his son very gravely. "All I ask is that you send me to Persia in the guise of a bride with a following suitable to my supposed estate. Have no fear that I shall not return in due course, and that I shall readily enough disembarrass myself of this avid Shah who seeks wives from the ends of the earth."

And so the Sultan was perforce compelled to leave the matter in this case. The Prince was provided with the richest feminine apparel that the principality could muster, jewels, silks, and muslins which the chief Sultana of the Commander of the Faithful herself might have envied. And on the tenth day from that on which the scheme was first mooted, Prince Musa set off for Isfahan, the capital of Persia, with a suite which made the peoples of the intervening provinces stare in sheer amazement. Yet every man in the train had been sworn to secrecy concerning the plan on pain of death.

And in due time the train reached the ancient and princely city of Isfahan, where the "Princess" and her suite were received with royal honours. And straightway she was brought to the Shah, where he sat in state in the great marble and golden palace of his ancestors. As Musa approached the throne with the grace of a gazelle, his face hidden beneath a cloud of veiling muslin, the Shah started and sat erect, clutching the jewelled arms of his great chair. Here indeed was beauty of form! Compared with such a shape the other princesses who had been sent in tribute seemed clumsy and bucolic. A very *houri*, he would swear!

So, after formal greeting, he invited Musa to the apartments in the harem which had been arranged for the reception of the Princess of Azerbaijan, and himself conducted him thence. And hardly had the threshold been crossed when he said:

"Fairest Princess—for that such a divine form is not accompanied by a most lovely countenance, I cannot believe—deign to unveil and display the transcendant beauty of your face to your fortunate lord."

With a great show of modesty which well pleased the Shah, Musa slowly, tantalizingly raised the folds of muslin which shrouded his face. And when the Shah gazed upon him, feasting his eyes on the peach-like skin, the ruby mouth, and the large and lustrous eyes, his heart beat quickly, and his breath came and went in little sobs, so beautiful was the seeming maiden.

"O miracle of loveliness, pearl of the earth," he panted, "grant that our nuptials be celebrated without delay."

"Sire," whispered Musa, veiling his eyes with their long lashes, "my desire is your Majesty's. But there is one vow I have made to myself, a sacred vow, that the man who weds me must first defeat me in wrestling. Bear with me, sire, but so it is, and, as you well know, such an oath cannot be broken."

Now the Shah laughed loudly, for he was the strongest and most skilful wrestler in all his dominions. But he was knowledgeable in the whims of womankind, and much too wise to thwart them.

"Charming Princess," he said, "your resolve is surely a strange one, yet have I heard vows even more fantastic. When is it your pleasure that we wrestle?"

"Whenever your Majesty pleases," answered Musa, dropping his veil.

"Now," thought the Shah, "it will be the quickest way to hold this paragon in my arms," and then aloud, "Why not at once, Princess?"

"As your Majesty chooses," murmured Musa demurely.

So at the Shah's bidding a wrestling mattress was brought in, and the combatants prepared themselves. The Shah stripped to the waist, his great muscles rising on his chest like brown ropes. But as for Musa, his breast remained covered, although his arms were bare, and he tucked the ample red silk trousers he wore up to the knee.

"Now," said the Shah with a smile, and the pair locked arms. It seemed the sorriest farce. Laughing, the Shah playfully tried to raise Musa in his arms—and found himself lying on his back.

He rose with a puzzled frown. "Surely this is black art," he complained. "Where Princess, did you learn such a trick?"

"Sire," said Musa, "you were not sufficiently on your guard. Try again."

The Shah, supposing he had slipped, engaged again, and this time with more caution. Indeed, he grasped Musa in such an umpleasantly ardent hold that the Prince gasped for breath. So he trampled as sharply as he could on the Shah's instep. The Shah, in agony with the pain, released his hold, whereupon the crafty Musa dived to the floor, caught the royal ankles firmly, and threw the Persian monarch to the mattress with such force that he lay unconscious.

The royal eunuchs, scandalised at what had occurred, hurried to their master's aid. They held perfumes to his nostrils and shook him gently, but it was not until Musa vigorously rubbed his ears that he came to himself again.

The Shah sat up and laid a hand tenderly on the back of his head. "By Allah!" he whispered, "are all the maidens of Azerbaijan like to you?"

By this time Musa had resumed his veil, and bowed low as she answered demurely: "Most, Sire, are far stronger and more skilful than I . I have seven sisters, any one of whom looks much more manly than I," which was precisely the truth.

"Thanks to the Compassionate One that I did not marry them all," remarked the Shah piously.

"But, Sire, you have not yet married me," said Musa, "nor is it possible for you to do so in face of my vow until you defeat me in wrestling."

"Umph," said the Shah rather sourly, "we will leave that for another day, Princess. For the present, however, it will prove much too dull for you to be shut up in apartments of your own, so I propose that you take up your quarters in my seraglio."

Now the Shah, in making this proposal, considered himself exceedingly clever, but it was precisely the move which Musa wished him to make. However, he dissembled.

"What, your Majesty," he cried, as if dreadfully shocked. "Your seraglio, according to the Persian custom, is a habitation for your wives alone, and I am neither your wife, nor yet one of that subsidiary class which"—here he wound his veil more tightly round his head—"scarcely rank as wives."

But the Shah was angry with the Princess whom he had sworn to humiliate because he had been beaten at his favourite sport. It was his intention to inveigle her into his harem, and to compel her to remain there as a mere concubine. If she attempted any of her wrestling tricks, well, his eunuchs would soon put an end to that.

"Your suspicions are unworthy of you, fair Princess," he said haughtily. "In my seraglio you will be as safe as in your father's palace," and without more ado he conducted her to the great house where his five hundred wives and women lived.

This was a terrible place, and that any man who was not a Shah or a Sultan could have tolerated such an atmosphere it is difficult to believe. For continual tumult reigned there as though it were a great cage of cockatoos or macaws. But an odd thing befell at the entrance of Musa, for everyone of the five hundred dames and damsels without exception at once grew profoundly quiet, so that as he trod the luxurious carpets of the gilded place one might have heard the dropping of a hairpin.

This, of course, the Shah took for mere curiosity, so dull are men, even princes of the greatest power and experience. And as it was the custom of the women to unveil at the advent of their liege lord, these five hundred matchless beauties, the pearls of the East, dark, brunette, fair, plump or slender, divinely tall or daintily petite, Persian, Afghan, Circassian, Arab or Egyptian, all turned their star-like gaze on the still-shrouded form of Musa with such expressions of envy (or so the Shah took it to be) that he chuckled in his beard and rubbed his great hands together in glee.

"Ah, ah," thought he, "patience, my moon-faced ones, and you shall behold a spectacle which will turn your hearts to little pits of hatred." Then with an obeisance to the Princess of Azerbaijan, he requested her to unveil.

With a regal movement, the swathing muslin was thrown back, and the result of this gesture thoroughly non-plussed the Shah. He had expected a murmurous outburst of envious criticism, but when a deep and prolonged sigh resounded from five hundred pairs of ruby lips, he was utterly at a loss.

From the throne where reclined the favourite to the balconies above, where the choicest beauties of the Orient were clustered like flowers, aye, to the farthest alcove of the great gilded hall, that sigh re-echoed in a perfervid moan of longing which baffled him. Yet there were many ladies present who in mere rapturous beauty could readily surpass the newcomer. True it was that none could boast of the exceeding grace of the Princess of Azerbaijan, none was her match in deportment and vivacity of movement, which were probably due to her skill and practice in athletics, and he trusted that her presence in the seraglio might provoke an emulation in carriage and activity which had hitherto been somewhat lacking among ladies who seemed to prefer lolling on heaped-up cushions to movement of any kind.

Smilingly he took his farewell of the Princess, and left the seraglio. No sooner had he gone than every woman it contained rushed to surround the newcomer and ply her with questions. She must sit beside the Princess of Trelijand, she must share the comfits of the black-browed beauty from Damascus, the grapes and medlars of the Circassian damsel were hers for the asking.

The seraglio was in an uproar. In vain the eunuchs strove to keep order. The Greeks swore that Musa was especially their friend, because "she" was fair; they placed garlands on his head and covered his arms with bracelets. The Egyptians, who believed in colour contrasts, wound their lithe arms round his neck, and snuggled their brown cheeks to his. Angered, the Greek maidens slapped the brown arms. The Egyptians returned scratches for the slaps and clung to their new acquaintance desperately. In the struggle Musa's dress became disarranged at the throat. A girl from Alexandria and another from Bessarabia both noticed at once that the breast of the Princess of Azerbaijan was covered with soft golden down, soft but thick. This, far from appearing as a disadvantage in a new lady friend, seemed to make them more anxious than ever to make her closer acquaintance, so that in the end poor Musa was all but smothered among the rarest female charms in the world.

But other than Greek and Egyptian damsels had a shrewd eye for the turn of events. The eunuchs had also observed the deshabille of the Princess and what it revealed, and took hurried counsel with one another. The Shah must be told. That he would be enraged they could scarcely doubt, but told he must be. So the Chief Eunuch went sadly to tell him.

When all was said, the Shah sat on his throne glaring at the Chief Eunuch like a lion in his wrath. Then by degrees his face softened, his eyes wrinkled in a smile, and he roared aloud. So loudly did he roar in his glee that the Chief Eunuch, thinking he was exceedingly angry, cast himself on his face and resigned himself to death.

There was a long pause. Then the Shah said mysteriously: "Bring the Princess of Azerbaijan before me." And when at last Musa was brought, the Shah looked upon him long and shrewdly.

"O most charming Princess," he said slowly, "I have considered the matter of our marriage with pious care, and although I rate your beauty and virtue most highly, it does not seem good to me that a wife should be a better wrestler than her husband. True, no man can say that there is in the Book aught against such an accomplishment in a spouse; only it does not appear seemly to me that as ruler of this great realm I should take to wife one who can so easily overthrow me. Moreover, although your beauty of feature cannot be gainsaid, I have learned that your bosom is as hirsute as that of a young man—a decided blemish in one so comely. Taking everything together, then, I judge it best that you should return with all speed to Azerbaijan, where, doubtless, your peculiar type of beauty is more appreciated. And so I bid you farewell."

And Musa, thinking of how he had thrown the Shah, put the leagues between himself and Isfahan at a speed quite surprising in one so ladylike.

*   *   *

Our first night in Syria saw the emergence of the talents

hidden within the beetle-browed head of our Pathan frontier companion, son of a chief of the mighty Afridi clan. Those who know these men of the Free Land, whom nobody has subdued in recorded history, will not be surprised that he spoke of chivalry and revenge: the contrast of this story with the last is a good example of the different mentality of the Persian and the Central Asian.

THE FARANGI PAYS HIS DEBT

The fact that Hamid Kahn had just finished his prayers (said the Afridi) did not deter him from planning vengeance, for a man cannot carry revenge in his heart for long without its becoming a part of himself, and Hamid Khan had already waited for two years. "Of a truth, by the hoof of the Evil One," he muttered to himself, "as an opportunity has not occurred, so I will create one, and make my way to the land of the *Farangis*, the Franks, who, unfortunately, but little appreciate my noble calling, and care not to welcome me in their land."

True it was that he had not been too well treated the last time he had ventured beyond the safety of his own hills into Peshawar, where he had perforce been obliged to go for a rifle, so dear to the hearts of the men who live in the Free Land beyond the Khyber. There is an explanation for most things, and the fact that the owner had given his life as well as his weapon was sufficient for anyone whose calling differed from that of this Frontier man. "But what did it matter about the Farangi anyway," thought he, "he is one less, and I would that he had been the one who murdered my brother Habib Khan, on whom be peace. Was it not such an one who killed my brother after calling him a pig, the worst insult to a Pathan, and one that can only be wiped out in blood."

It was vengeance for this, then, that Hamid Khan thirsted. "Time hangs heavily on these hands of mine," he murmured to himself, "and I would have things out with the Farangi Captain who lives in the land of Hindustan." And the Pathan touched his Afghan knife lovingly. "Of a truth will I go to that land of pestilence as a trader. So will I find this Frank, for as a trader none will suspect my intention, and by the help of Allah will I square the deal with the Kaffir infidel." After which comforting thought Hamid Khan drew a hissing breath and spat forcefully to relieve his feelings. "It is a way after mine own heart," he said chuckling in his beard, for the Captain must think the affair long forgotten, while the privilege of remembering is mine!" He arose, put away his *hookah* pipe, adjusted his turban, and taking his stick, proceeded to the village market, where he spent a few of his scanty store of rupees on some rugs, which he hoisted on his shoulder, smiling all the while at his shrewdness. "These rugs will stand me well in the land of the Franks who fly devil machines and eat pigs. Not a hint shall I drop to my kinsmen, lest my purpose fail and I become the butt and jest of every beardless youth in the village."

Difficulties as to road expenses might arise, but it was only to outward appearance that Hamid Khan was a peaceful trader. No one knew better, when necessity arose, how to extract rupees from the Hindu moneylenders, wary and otherwise. So the fact that his money-belt was uncomfortably empty caused neither discontent nor discouragement to him. Grasping his stout stick he set forth along the hill road with the easy stride of a man accustomed to walking long distances. The rugs dangled over his left shoulder, a mixture of happiness and revenge was in his heart, and the words Allah-o-Akbar (God is great) were on his lips. From time to time he met fat *bunias* (moneylenders) making their way in their usual ponderous gait to collect outstanding monies due to them. It must have been for a considerable sum, for only in these circumstances did the ease-loving usurers care to brave the perils that await such as they in the narrow and danger-fraught hill passes. These Shylocks cast uneasy glances at the big Pathan with the best of good reasons. But Hamid Khan was not in pressing necessity, and perhaps on the return journey, having, by the help of Allah, disposed of his enemy, he would naturally want to commemorate the occasion by giving a feast in his village. If he had his usual good fortune this would coincide with the return of the *bunia* with a few fat bags of rupees.

So, for many days, Hamid Khan travelled in peace through the hills, and down through the boulder-strewn passes where a blade of grass is as rare as water in the desert. Eventually he arrived in India, the goal of his undertaking. "I will eat now," spoke the Frontiersman to himself, when he eventually sat in the Bazaar at Peshawar, "for I have the feeling of emptiness which does not make for comfort." Swarthy hillmen strode through the Bazaar chewing dried figs and buying mulberries all the way from Afghanistan. Here and there Uzbeks in long felt boots and fur hats from far-off Turkestan wended their way through the crowds. Everyone parted readily with his money in this land of plenty.

As he sat eating rice cooked in Pathan fashion, some old comrades of past lurid exploits passed near him on their way through the Bazaar. They would have welcomed an exchange of confidences with their old friend, but one look from him intimated that it was not an auspicious moment to renew acquaintanceship, and no further recognition took place. Well they knew they would hear the story in the near future in the peace and hospitality of their own hills, where there was no danger attached to the asking of questions. Having eaten, Hamid Khan rose to his feet. "Now will I proceed to the dwelling of the Frank, which will be of a situation greatly different to that of the men of Hindustan whom the Inglis have conquered these many years!" Hamid Khan laughed the carefree laugh of the hillman.

He left the Bazaar and made his way through the city to the Military Cantonment. "Of a surety these Franks well know the ways of comfort and pleasure," he remarked to himself as he approached a large bungalow. "They have taken soft ways much to the heart."

Just at that crucial moment further ruminations were cut short by the approach of two military policemen, who came towards him in anything but a friendly manner.

"What are you doing here?" one asked him in the native language. "Yesterday we thought we had rounded up every Pathan within a radius of ten miles after they raided the Bazaar the night before, and if here isn't one at large under our very noses."

"I know nothing of what you speak," replied Hamid, "I am but a poor trader, whose only desire is to sell a few rugs to the Sahibs in the bungalows here and return home."

"Not on your life," said one of the British policemen, at which both laughed. "Hand over the old blunderbuss and come with us." Obediently Hamid Khan handed over his heavy stick. His wrists were handcuffed and as he marched along the baking road between his captors his heart sank. Was this, then, to be the end of the opportunity: just as success had

71

presented itself?

A few moments more saw him inside the cell of a wayside prison. The door clanged behind him and his activities, so far as the outside world was concerned, were at an end. He gazed longingly at the bungalows from the iron-barred window. "Fool that I was not to wait until nightfall, for the darkness hath ever been a good friend to me. It is well that I mentioned not this plan of mine to the village folk, for their jokes would have brought the taste of bitterness to this mouth of mine!"

His captors, two officious-looking English soldiers, kept inside the shady veranda opposite, while the sun shone straight through the barred window of the prison cell. "Of what do these Farangis talk?" wondered the captive, as the policemen laughed loudly. "Would that positions were changed and that these captors were at my mercy in mine own hills. Laugh they might, but it would only be if they enjoyed my hospitality!" The thought of how he would like to entertain the guards under the changed circumstances was too much for Hamid Khan, he forgot his predicament and laughed with vigour. "Lummy!" ejaculated one of the policemen, "Is he barmy?" Then turning to his companion he said, "You bet he feels the heat as bad as we do." And here he went over to the cell and broke the rules of the prison by handing a cigarette to the Pathan.

That night there was no sleep for the prisoner in the hot discomfort of the narrow cell, and day brought the merciless heat of the sun, which at noon shone once more on the prisoner. "Allah-o-Akbar," cried the Pathan as he lay on the floor, minus coat, shoes and turban. Just then some Army officers came and looked in at him. A long conversation took place between them and the guards, and when the officers rode away one of the policemen spoke to the prisoner at the grating. "You are to get out tomorrow, Miller Sahib says so, and you had better beat it after that, my lad, or you might have a dusty time if we catch you again." But the last sentence was lost on Hamid Khan. All the gathered vengeance of the last two years rose before him. In an instant he was on his feet, the lethargy gone, the heat forgotten. Although he was in the grip of rage and great excitement his voice showed no emotion as he said, "This Miller Sahib must be a great soldier when a word of his can excuse a prisoner who sees no way of escape."

"Yes," came the reply, on every word of which the frontiers-man hung, "he is in the Frontier Rifles, that is his bungalow over there with the wall round it. He used to know your God-forsaken part of the country well."

"Ah!" the ejaculation was a mixture of relief and returned hope. "Miller Sahib of the Frontier Rifles! The murderer of my brother Habib Khan!" thought the hillman. "It is well to have suffered so to have the prey delivered into mine hands! Allah-o-Akbar!" Never had the Pathan uttered the words with such reverence, or so great belief in their truth.

That night there was little sleep for Hamid Khan, for the excitement at being so close to his prey was as new life to the man. The discomfort was forgotten; nothing but tomorrow's freedom and what it meant was in his mind. Next day he was free and lost no time in getting to the bungalow of Captain Miller. Entering the compound he went to the kitchen quarters.

"Salaam-alaikum" (Peace be on you), he said to the cook. "Does your master require such poor services as I can offer?"

"The Sahib is away," replied the cook. "He has much work of great importance to do, and will not return until to-night, when he has a *burra khana* (dinner party), but he requires a *chowkidar* (night-watchman) and if it is not too long for you to wait, I think you can be sure of the job. The Sahib has much money and gives good pay."

"I will wait," replied Hamid Khan, who thought that a few hours were as nothing compared to the last two years.

That night saw him in his new role of *chowkidar* to the Englishman. The rest was only the matter of a few hours. Many times he walked round the bungalow, as was his duty. The dinner party was in full swing, and the Captain had just given him some orders, adding that if a message came for him during the night it would be important and was to be given to him at once. The infidel would be retiring soon, thought Hamid Khan. "I shall rest for an hour, for the last few nights have unnerved me, and I would have a steady hand, for tonight calls for one."

He awoke some time later with a start. "Fool that I am," murmured the frontiersman, "how long have I slept, and what is the hour? Lucky it is that it is still dark." A clock struck the hour of 2 a.m. All was silent. Even the seemingly tireless jackals held their peace. "The hour is come!" muttered Hamid Khan.

"Strength to my sword arm! Now will I challenge and slay the Farangi ere cock crow, and the father of the man who will capture Hamid Khan under circumstances so auspicious has yet to learn the art of walking!"

Slipping off his sandals, the Pathan made his way noiselessly along the veranda to the Captain's bedroom. The night was hot and the glass door had been left open as is the custom. It was the work of a few seconds to slip aside the grass *chick* (blind) and creep into the bedroom. The frontiersman found himself in a large room, in which a dim light showed in a distant corner. Drawing his long Afghan blade he approached the bed.

"Son of a dog!" he said in a gruff whisper, "behold in me Hamid Khan, the avenger of my brother Habib Khan! Arise, murderer! and strike thy *tulwar* blade on mine, for either thou or I shall die! Sit up, for I kill not any man while he lies asleep!" There was no sound from the bed and Hamid repeated the challenge. As he said the last words a form rose in the bed, and to his amazement Hamid Khan saw the figure of a woman. He drew back.

"A woman!" he cried, "Do mine eyes behold a woman? What is this? Art thou a ghost? an *afrit?* Speak!"

"I am no ghost," came the reply in steady tones, "I am a woman."

"Where is the Captain?"

"I do not know." Again the reply showed no sign of fear. Terror seized the hillman. There was something mysterious in the situation. Perhaps Allah in his desire to save the life of the Englishman had changed him to woman's form.

"It cannot be that these eyes of mine play me false," reasoned the Pathan, terrified at what other mystery might overtake him in this land of darkness. Hamid Khan, whose name for bravery was known on all the broad Frontier, frightened by a woman! He hastened on, and dawn saw him well on his way out of the land of the unbelievers.

Eight days later he arrived home to find the place almost in ruins. Huge branches from the mulberry trees were strewn in confusion everywhere, great dark stains on the ground showed more clearly than any words could have done, what had happened. The thatched roofs had been burned, and the watch-tower was dismantled. The unaccustomed silence sent a shudder of fear through the heart of the Pathan, fear as to the safety of his aged father. He hurried to his home, where he found his father alive but suffering from severe wounds and grief at the death of his youngest son who had been killed in his sight. It appeared that a neighbouring Chief had renewed an old quarrel and taken the village unawares, so that the father and his followers had had more than enough to do to defend themselves. As luck would have it some British soldiers, newly arrived, and stationed only a short distance away, came to the old man's aid. He continued for long in glowing terms of the bravery of the soldiers, and especially of the leader, who defended the wounded old man at great peril to his own life. The Captain, leader of the soldiers, lay now in hospital so badly wounded that he might not recover.

"Long have I spat at the sight of a Frank, O my son," spoke his father, "but Allah hath shown me the error of hatred in mine old age, for had we been alone we should surely have been killed in thine absence."

When the old man recovered sufficiently he and Hamid Khan went to the hospital to thank the Englishman for his assistance and to enquire how he was progressing. When they reached the bedside both men were moved to pity, for the man lying there was swathed in bandages and only one eye was visible. He was too weak from loss of blood to talk, and the visitors were asked to leave after a few moments. The next time they went to the hospital the patient had improved, and talking was allowed. During the conversation the Captain said that when he felt he was dying an incident hung heavily on his conscience, and that he would now like to ease his mind by relating it to the visitors.

Haltingly and with difficulty the Captain told of how he had accidently shot one of their countrymen. Two years ago he had employed a Pathan as night-watchman. One night returning from the Club, where he had had too much to drink, he found the *chowkidar* asleep, instead of attending to his duties. He called the man a pig, the worst insult for a Pathan, and the punishment for which by Hill-law is death. But the Pathan, having eaten the salt of the Captain, gave the latter the chance to take back his words. The Englishman was not in his right senses and repeated the insult. The *chowkidar* snatched his knife

75

and rushed at the Captain, who drew his revolver in self-defence. The two closed and struggled. The gun went off, and the Pathan rolled to the ground. He was dead.

Silence reigned in the whitewashed ward of the little hospital. Hamid Khan stroked his beard. "And the name of the *chowkidar*?" he demanded with emphasis on every word. "Habib Khan," came the reply.

"Knowest thou that he was mine own brother and dearer to me than my right hand? Dost thou know that I have carried hatred for thee in mine heart for two whole years until, like a burning fire, it consumed me and the only ease mine spirit knew was the plan I made to destroy thee? It was to carry out this that I braved the perils and travelled into the land of Hindustan to crush the life out of thee with these hands of mine. For the hate I bore thee was as great as the love I had for mine own brother. With difficulty I reached Peshawar and obtained work as a *chowkidar* in thy service. That night thou toldst me of the urgent message. I know now that thou wert called away from there. But I knew it not then, and made my way to thy room to kill thee, and so avenge my brother. On reaching thy room I was afraid when a woman appeared, when I expected only thee, and I thought that Allah saw fit to preserve thy life by changing thee to the form of a woman. I fled, for a Pathan does not kill women." The brigand's voice rose again and again as he related the story of his hatred. Now, placing his head between both hands, he said, "Thanks be to Allah that thy life was spared and for thy noble defence of my old father who is more dear to me than anything on this earth. My affection for him is greater than my hate for thee. Thus by saving him thou hast paid the debt. Take this turquoise ring from my finger, and if ever thou shouldst be in danger from any of my clansmen show it, and it will assure thee passage in safety where no other infidel dare go. In this wise I prove thee that instead of the great hate I bore thee, gratitude only remains in the heart of Hamid Khan."

*　　　*　　　*

Now, in the East there is a question: are the Pathans like the Kurds, or are the Kurds like the Pathans? It was therefore no surprise to any of us, one weary halt-time, when Haji Ibrahim

Naqshbandi, Kurdish chieftain and seasoned traveller of the Arabian deserts, who looked like a swashbuckling candidate for a warlike epic film, claimed his right to recount an adventure which befell him when he was last in these very parts, returning from a pilgrimage. Amazingly, he was an amateur archaeologist, too.

THE SHEIK, THE SON, AND THE SACK

On this particular trip, he said, I was the guest of a sheik. I shall not mention his name. It will not be safe for you, for he shoots before speaking. He was a good enough host though; his whole camel-hair tent and his entire rations were placed at my disposal, for Arab hospitality is real as well as proverbial.

He had only one joke, this sheik. "Ah, you Ajami," he would say. For to the Arabs, all the rest of the world is Ajam, which is not Arab. It means 'dumb'. He would show a tooth like a jackal's, and laughed at the idea that we Kurds could be of any use to the world.

I met the sheik in the oddest way. I was riding camel-back from Maabilah, hoping to make Baalbek. I am not going to hand you out the old mossy tale about an eclipse of the sun, but it *did* just happen that one came along that very afternoon.

A shadow like the edge of a big bad penny began to creep across the disc of day. Of course, I saw at once what it was, and cursed. The beastly thing would last for over a couple of hours, and, as it threatened to grow pitch dark, I would perforce have to dismount. Hard cheese, when I had figured to be at Baalbek by five o'clock.

Suddenly a bombardment like a second-class battle flared to the south of me. On the other side of one of the big sandhills men were shooting like mad, and giving vent to the most bloodthirsty yells.

With the proverbial curiosity of my race I spurred my *heri* to the top of the mound and looked down. Some half-dozen Arabs were blazing away at the sky. On seeing me they stopped and, jumping on their camels, rode quickly to the summit of the rise.

"What are you firing at?" I asked. "Airplanes?"

"No, no," irritably shouted a big man whom I took for the leader. "Can't you see? *Sheitan*, Satan, he's swallowing the sun. We're firing at him to make him stop."

"Waste of powder, my friend," I laughed. "There's no

Sheitan there. It's only an eclipse and you know what that is surely?"

"If you're trying to hocus me with any of your modern stuff," he shouted, "You'd better think again, for I'm not having any."

"If that's Sheitan," I asked, pointing to the now very apparent shadow on the luminary, "where are his teeth? You are duffers, you desert Arabs. Can't you see that's only the shadow of the moon? It'll disappear in an hour or two, as it always does. Surely you've seen an eclipse before without making all this hullabaloo about it?"

"Of course we've seen it before," answered the sheik; "but in the other cases it only disappeared because we fired at it."

And suiting the action to the word, he raised his long rifle and banged away at the orb of day, imitated by his faithful servitors.

"How many millions of miles off do you think it is?" I asked. "Easy to see you never got *The Story of the Heavens* as a school prize."

But I let them carry on without further argument, for, thinking of my own personal safety, I concluded it would be just as well that they should exhaust their ammunition.

This they very soon did, while the light faded into almost total darkness. When they had expended their last bullets the chief turned to me.

"Fire, can't you," he commanded, but I shook my head.

"We're economical folk, we Kurdish Persians," I said. "I'm not wasting any Mauser bullets on Old Man Sol."

"So you're an Irani?" laughed the sheik. "Of course, that explains a lot. Where are you bound for?"

"Baalbek. I'm going to write about it."

This statement was greeted with respectful silence. The desert Arab has an enormous veneration for anyone who can write.

"We are going in that very direction," said the Sheik. "You will not, however, reach Baalbek tonight for there are bandits in the pass. But I can offer you entertainment. Even if you are an *Ajami* dumb foreigner you're a Moslem of sorts. Come along."

As I was the only man there with any ammunition left, I didn't mind going along, but I resolved to keep my eyes skinned, for the gang looked rather an unreliable lot, and I didn't particularly want to wake up with the Sign of the Crescent across my throat. We rode for miles in almost absolute silence over the sands and gradually the light returned. At length we came to a fairly large encampment, which seemed to consist chiefly of tents, goats and smell.

We dismounted and the sheik conducted me to his tent. Conducted is good, for in reality we had to crawl in it. His harem was divided from the living apartment by a screen of camel-hair cloth swarming with flies, but he ordered some quite passable coffee from a black slave, and handed me a *chibuq* filled with excellent Anatolian tobacco.

"Listen," he said, "when you depart on the morrow I want you to do me a favour."

I indicated that I would be happy to oblige him if it wasn't anything too embarrassing.

"It's just to carry a sack of corn to a friend of mine at the mouth of the pass," he assured me with a wink.

"Sack of corn, why?" I laughed. "Hasn't your friend any breadstuffs of his own? What's all the mystery about, anyhow?"

The sheik laughed too. "Oh, you Ajamis," he roared, "you are such funny fellows."

"Someone's told you that twenty years ago and you've evidently never got over it," I said rudely, for all this jeering at my race was beginning to get on my nerves.

"It's all right, brother," he giggled. "Don't get angry. Now, see here. Karim, the son of my friend the Sheik Abdul, got lost in the desert, and he offered a reward of two camels for the boy's recovery. I have found the lad. The camels came to hand yesterday morning. Naturally I must now send the imp of Eblis back to his sire."

"But why in a sack?" I said.

"Well, if he's not tied up, he'll jump off your animal at once, you see. Will you do it?"

"Well, since you've given me your hospitality I can't refuse, can I? All the same I don't much like the job. Looks as though you'd kidnapped the little beggar yourself."

"It's really nothing," he assured me, "just carrying a sack on the hind-hump of your *heri* for an hour or two."

We ate, and after more coffee and tobacco, went to bed, or what passes for bed in an Arab tent.

I dozed off almost at once, and must have been asleep for several hours, when I was rudely awakened by the sound of a shot.

"What in the name of Allah . . .?" I began, sitting up quickly enough.

"It's all right," barked the sheik. "That infernal slave of mine, son of Eblis, tried to bag your binoculars, and I shot him, that's all. It's a pity, for he made such good coffee."

"Good heavens," I cried, "you don't mean to say you killed the poor devil just for that? Where is he?"

"Just outside," laughed the sheik. "But why do you want to know?"

I dragged the unfortunate slave in and found he was slightly wounded in the leg. I bound it up as well as I could in the circumstances.

There wasn't much more sleep that night, for the sheik kept me awake with his laughter at the vagaries of the Kurds. Why on earth should anyone worry about a slave or two? He passed from one fit of cachinnation to another. And then he began to snore, giggling every now and again in his sleep.

At last came daybreak and I made a job of the slave's leg and left him some dressings and antiseptic, which he promised, in a bewildered sort of way, to use. Then we breakfasted and the sheik produced the boy whom I was to take to his father at the mouth of the pass in the Anti-Lebanon mountains.

When I saw the young shaver I had misgivings.

"It is seven miles to the mouth of the pass," said the sheik, "and it is now bandit-proof, as I've ascertained. All the same, you'd better keep under the shadow of the hillside as much as possible. Got everything you want?"

"As man to man, sheik," I asked, "is there any catch in this?"

"I assure you that everything's straight and above board," replied the sheik, looking me fairly between the eyes. "It is not in my heart to lie to you."

"Well, I'll take your word for it", I said; "but remember, if there's any hanky-panky about this I'll come back—and I won't come back alone."

For answer the sheik merely spread out his hands in a deprecatory gesture. I drummed my heels on my camel's ribs

81

and started, the sack, with boy complete, bobbing at my rear.

We hadn't gone half-a-mile when that infernal young limb of Sheitan began to make such a hubbub that I was compelled to stop. He wailed like a banshee, but what he said I couldn't hear, for the sack muffled his words.

"Look here, my young friend," I shouted, vigorously shaking the bundle in which he was tied, "stop that song and dance inside there, or I'll chuck you off and leave you to be eaten by the vultures."

This speech drew a louder howl than ever, although never a word could I make out of what the brat said—I knew why later. But resolving to take no notice, I rode on. I quickly covered the two or three miles to the mouth of the pass, which, as the sheik had assured me, seemed to have not a single bandit left in its bounds, and came, rather too suddenly for me, on the village of the local big-wig Abdul, whose son and heir I was conveying home.

And only then did it strike me—dolt that I had been—that something was wrong in the arrangements!

Alas, it was too late to retrace my tracks, for just as the oddity of the thing was striking me, a round dozen of Arabs suddenly appeared as if from the sand, and surrounded me.

"What do you want here *effen?*" asked one, who evidently took me for a Turk. "You can't collect taxes nowadays, you know."

"Nothing doing in that way, brother," I said, as cheerily as I could. "I've brought the sheik's son home. Can I see his worship at once?"

It wasn't necessary to inquire further. At that moment the Sheik Abdul came running out of his tent. I introduced myself with all the formality suitable to such an occasion, and told him of my errand. In another second he was pulling at the goatskin thongs which bound up the mouth of the sack, blaspheming lustily the while and muttering endearments.

"Karim, jewel of the desert," he cried, "hast thou then returned to thy father at last? And, wherefore has this monster of cruelty brought thee back to me in a foul sack, smelling of the produce of the Franks, the *Feringhees?* Rest assured that he shall suffer for the affront, my little star, my lambkin."

Now this didn't sound any too reassuring, and I began to

finger my gun.

"Sheik Abdul," I said, "I'm merely a messenger. I had nothing to do whatever with the affair I . . ."

"Hold thy peace," cried Abdul in a white fury. "Do you see those black flags fluttering on the sandhills yonder?"

"Aye, sheik, I see them. What of them?"

"What of them! He asks what of them," howled Abdul, tugging at the thongs in a frenzy. "Here, Turk, thy knife."

"With pleasure, sheik, but I'm no Turk. I'm a Kurd."

"A wha-a-t?" bellowed the sheik, "a Kurd did you say?"

"What's the matter?" I asked lamely.

"He asks what's the matter," screamed Abdul. "Look dog, see the black flags?"

"Less of the dog stuff," I growled, drawing my revolver. "You're behaving like a fool, sheik. I don't get you at all."

"The black flags," murmured one of the suite, "mean that the sheik's beautiful daughter was abducted yesterday. Unhappily, the abductor chanced to be a Kurd."

"And if one camel bites you, do you thrash another camel?" I asked sententiously.

But my old-time illustration was drowned in a series of maledictions, for by this time the sheik had unbound the mouth of the sack and had drawn forth its occupant, who had been gagged. Howls rent the air.

"By all the fiends of Eblis," yelled the sheik, "this is not Karim."

"Not . . . your son!" I cried in a strangled voice.

"That spawn of a spavined dromedary my son!" spluttered Abdul. "Seize that robber of children!"

"Look here, sheik," I said, brandishing my hand gun, "I can make every allowance for your grief and disappointment as a father, but if you try on any funny business, you're apt to swallow some sand. Now, look here. If you'll return with me to the home of your kidnapping neighbour, we'll soon put things to rights."

"I'm going there at once," replied the sheik with horrid calm, "as soon as I've impaled you and this devil's offspring here."

"Oh, if it's like that," I said sternly, "let's begin the impaling now. But there'll be some plugging first."

Abdul looked somewhat alarmed. "Be it as you say," he croaked angrily, "but if I do not recover my son, beware."

We mounted with the yelling brat before me, and sped up the pass again.

In a little more than an hour our fast-trotting camels carried us over the rocky road. We were just in time, for the sheik and his henchmen were in the act of striking camp.

"Accursed one," yelled Abdul, "where is my son?"

"Produce that boy," I shouted, handing him the counterfeit monkey, "or, by Sheitan, it's your last morning, you dirty kidnapper."

The sheik looked dazed. "What's the matter?" he said in amazement. "I don't know what you're talking about. Put away that gun, Kurd. I don't like the look of it."

Abdul hurled himself upon the sheik and seized him by the throat. The pair rolled over and over in the sand.

"Get up," I said, "and listen to reason. Sheik, where is Abdul's boy? Produce him at once, you wretched double-crosser—and the girl as well."

"The girl!" moaned the sheik, nursing his left eye, in which Abdul had inserted a probing thumb. "I can give you the boy, but there's no girl here."

"Liar," I said quietly, "You pinched Abdul's daughter yesterday and had it put about that I had done the job. So that's why you giggled in your sleep last night, eh? Now bring them both here before I start shooting."

Sulkily the sheik ambled to his tent, and after rummaging in the women's quarters, reappeared, driving before him a boy of some seven years and a girl who looked about sixteen.

They at once ran to Abdul who embraced them rapturously. Then he turned to the sheik.

"Jinn of the sand-hills," he hissed, "where are the camels I sent you?"

"The camels," said the Sheik lamely, "did you send camels? Well I suppose they'll be with the herd. I must be going. Business is slack about here."

"Take this with you," I said kicking him in the proper place with my heavy riding-boot, "and please understand that next time you meet a Kurd you can't do him down as you tried to do me."

As we rode off, a bullet or two whizzed past. I loosed a couple of shots, but the firing soon ceased.

The sheik turned to me. "Kurd," he said, with a noble air, "you are a hero. How I have misjudged you! But to make amends I shall bestow upon you my daughter's hand."

"Sorry, Abdul," I replied, "but I am already married."

"But do the Kurds not have more than one wife?" he asked in amazement.

"Not if we can help it," I assured him. "It's kind of you, very thoughtful indeed, but I must be getting on to Baalbek."

"To Baalbek! But there's nothing doing there . . ."

"There's the ruins, it is a nice, quiet spot . . ."

"The ruins!" murmured the Sheik. "Allah be good to him, for the poor Kurd is crazy after all!"

*   *   *

"The wrong person . . ." mused a wandering merchant from India. "Many interesting things can happen when we have people getting mixed up. I remember a case which occurred during my boyhood, in the far-off Punjab."

We pressed him to begin the tale, for on this particular day we had slept longer than usual, and the Caravan-Master had warned us that there was less than a hour to starting-time.

The Indian took a long breath and began.

BANDMASTER

'Sawni, the musician, had made the grade.

It had been a difficult and nerve-searing business, but he had won through.

He was now a bandmaster, and he possessed his own band.

True, it was he who played the big drum and Tilak, the inebriate, who had, in an alcoholic moment, undertaken to play the flute. That was the band.

Small, yes. But he prided himself on the fact that it would be good. There was no better drummer in the whole of the Punjab.

Moreover, big business would follow. For the time being he would have to rest content with a lowly place at the tail of marriage processions. Failing that, he would be required to displace the air with some mournful dirge at funerals of the poorer bazaar folk. The point was that he was now his own master. He was open for engagements.

For years he had trundled his drum in the imposing entourage of the boastful Larmi. That had been a good band. There was, or rather had been, the big drum, three flutes, two cornets, a bassoon (a trifle uncertain this as the performer was a *zemindar*, a smallholder, and had to till his field), sundry kettle-drums, and lastly, Larmi, who led the band upon a white horse. The horse, too, was uncertain at odd moments. It was owned by the bassoon player. Often it was required to pull the plough, and sometimes it was hired out. The bassoon player was a man of parts. He owned a livery stable. The white horse filled the role.

Larmi had done things in style. When he set up in business he had resolved that his band should be the big noise. His brother, a lascar on a great black and white liner, had been entrusted with a secret commission when next he should touch at Tilbury. The result had been a visit to an East End shopkeeper with a touch of humour and no conscience, and a collection of military head-dresses from the Scottish highlands as worn by a famous kilted regiment at the Crimean War.

Larmi was delighted. He considered that the family had obtained much for its money. The effect, when the headgear was superimposed upon shirts, the tails of which flapped outside pyjamas or dhoti, the nether garments depending upon the caste of the performer, was both striking and picturesque.

This ensemble was a wow in the bazaars and it brought Larmi many rupees.

Now Sawni had defected and he had handed in his uniform as a labourer might hand in his check.

Larmi had been surprised. Sawni had intended that he should be. He was a musician and an artist, and he was great on effects.

"Well, well," Larmi had said. "So you are leaving my fine band."

"Aye," Sawni responded airily. "I go to better myself."

"Larmi raised his eyebrows. "You give up the big drum?"

"No!" Sawni's great moment had arrived. "I have formed a band of my own."

"So-o! We are to be rivals, are we?"

Sawni smirked, unctuously.

"And this band. Who are they who will provide the music?"

Sawni swelled his chest. "I will play the big drum," he said, and paused.

"And—?"

"Tilak will play the flute."

"That old dodderer!"

"He is no dodderer. He is a fine artist."

"He is a fine drinker. He played for me once—the wrong tunes."

"That was your fault." Sawni had seen his chance and had taken it.

Larmi swelled with indignation. "My fault?" he asked, his voice shaking with anger.

"You were the bandmaster, weren't you?" Sawni put the question gently.

"You think that I cannot control a band?"

"I know that you cannot. I, with my big drum, have controlled your band for years. You have taken silver rupees—and you have rewarded me with copper pice."

"Imbecile!"

"Dodderer!"

Larmi and Sawni parted.

Then, as everywhere else, there came the depression.

Some bazaar folk still died and others continued to get married, but the moneylenders who are wont to finance such undertakings became canny. No longer was it possible to sign a bill for five hundred rupees and receive only three hundred at extortionate interest.

Sawni did well out of the slump. Those who, in more ordinary circumstances, would have despised his band, were forced to look for cheaper performers. Many deserted the grandiose Larmi and perforce engaged Sawni.

Sawni began to prosper. He found it possible to augment his instrumentalists. Tilak, the flautist, found that he had support in his wilder moments. This was provided by an attenuated youth with a cornet.

There followed an obese gentleman with a kettle-drum and then, as engagements continued to flow in, a wild man from the hills with a long Eastern Sitar.

This was the *pièce de resistance*. Sawni now had a band. It rose to giddy altitudes. It advanced from the bazaar version of "British Grenadiers," which for so long had comprised its entire repertoire, and essayed "The Campbells are Coming." Moreover, notwithstanding the slowness of the tempo and the amazing obligato contributed by Tilak the inebriate, someone even recognized the air.

This in itself was a compliment to the band's prowess, and Sawni was elated. Unfortunately, the matter came to the ears of Larmi who, smarting under many financial setbacks, immediately saw his opportunity of putting Sawni where he wanted him.

He repaired to the Small Cause Court in the depths of the bazaar. There a tout conveyed him into the presence of a gentleman of grave mien. The learned one had two small white linen tabs dangling at his collarless throat. These told the world that the wearer had been to the law college, and moreover had passed his examinations. In other words, he was an accredited pleader, or a small-time barrister.

This man of the law conducted his business with clients

under a tree in the court compound.

Here, sitting cross-legged, Larmi recounted his grievances. For years, he explained, he and his band had played the air of the Campbells, and now another band sought to rob him of his livelihood.

Larmi was solemnly informed that an action for infringement of copyright undoubtedly existed. What is more amazing, the small court judge, who still owed Larmi a bill in connection with the marriage of his third daughter, thought so too.

Sawni was informed that he was required to pay into court the sum of a hundred and fifty rupees as damages.

Sawni staggered under the blow, but he did not despair. The payment of damages robbed him of all his hard-earned capital, but he still had his band.

Also there was Ganesh Chand—Mr. Ganesh Chand—at whose house he was now a frequent visitor.

There were, of course, the Misses Chand. Occasionally, visitors to the house became aware of girlish giggles, but otherwise the young ladies comported themselves with due decorum.

Hence Sawni—and Larmi, for he refused to desert the picture.

Mr. Chand welcomed both, for he had two daughters, and both were liabilities. As far as possible, it was arranged that the swains should visit the house at different times.

The bazaar watched the manoevres with a cynical interest.

"Old Chand," it said, "is getting rid of his Loti at last."

"What of the other girl?" others would ask.

The bazaar would shrug its shoulders.

"Loti is the one," it would reply—" and two men are after her. And both are bandmasters—and rivals. Mark my words, there will be trouble."

The Bazaar observed the lugubrious countenance of Sawni and declared that the loss of his rupees had put a bias upon his chances. They took note of the smug expression of Larmi and opened a book on the outcome.

Sometimes Larmi and Sawni met, and they had words— bitter words. After one of these encounters, Larmi decided to take the plunge. He discussed finance with Mr. Chand. Loti, he discovered, had as her portion some three hundred rupees, sundry household chattels and an extensive wardrobe. He took the bait. He made but one stipulation, and that was that the contract should be kept from the ears of Sawni.

The marriage ceremony, he insisted, should not take place at the house of Mr. Chand, because that, though delightful as a bazaar residence, did not afford that accommodation necessary for the comfort of a concourse of guests.

Mr. Chand readily agreed. It meant a little more on the gross amount of the dowry, but, with a quick mental calculation, he decided that it was worth it.

So matters progressed. Larmi, immersed in the preparations for his forthcoming wedding, allowed engagement after engagement to go by. Sawni snapped them up. He more than made good his hundred and fifty rupees.

Finally he was engaged for a wedding—a big wedding—for his fee was to amount to thirty rupees.

Perched upon a veranda, half-hidden by palms, Sawni saw little of the ceremony. The occasion, however, was a great one and he exhorted his band to give of its best.

Tilak, the inebriate, under the effects of liberal libations, rendered the British Grenadiers with many a variation. Sawni perspired freely as he beat his drum The wild Pathan from the hills performed prodigies of instrumentation, while the cornet blew hard and long and filled in the gaps when the flautist was out of wind.

There came the time when the guests formed into a procession behind the bridal pair and the band was required to leave its sanctuary upon the veranda. Sawni led his men bravely forth and was confronted by an elated Larmi.

He held his veiled bride by the arm. He puffed out his cheeks imposingly.

"Ah, Sawni," he said patronisingly. "Thank you for the music."

Sawni stared.

Larmi looked on delightedly.

"Didn't you know that it was my wedding?" he asked.

Sawni remained silent.

"Look, he is struck dumb," roared Larmi.

Larmi turned to his bride. "Just lift your veil, little one," he said, "so that your face may be seen."

The girl at his side obeyed nervously.

"Look, just look!" bellowed Larmi, "It is Loti!" And he doubled up with laughter.

Sawni gazed at his adversary unmoved.

Larmi turned from laughter to anger.

"What," he cried, disappointed that the other should display such aplomb, "have you nothing to say?"

Sawni found his tongue. "Not here," he replied. "Not here," and he indicated the assembled guests. "Come beneath the trees," he invited, "and I will speak".

Out of the earshot of the company Larmi, the bellicose, turned on his companion. He panted as he spoke, for the ceremony had involved much eating and drinking. "Loti," he said. "Loti. Do you not see it is I who have married Loti?"

Sawni smiled. "I was never interested in Loti," he explained. "Her sister, though a year older, is a comely girl. Besides, your Loti has a temper—as you will find. And," went on Sawni impressively, "besides the dowry apportioned by her father, which is greater than that given with Loti, there is a rich endowment from an aunt—a small matter of eight hundred rupees."

Larmi gulped. He fought for words. They came with a rush. "Rogue," he raved. "And you will marry this girl?"

Sawni grinned, somewhat maliciously. "I have," he responded. "The ceremony was yesterday—it was very quiet."

Larmi clutched at his brow; a groan broke from his lips.

Gradually, the full realization of the calamity came upon him. He gazed weakly upon Sawni.

"So we—we are brothers-in-law," he faltered.

He staggered back to Loti.

*   *   *

This story so much interested the other travellers that they begged the merchant to tell them another. Thus it was that, at our next halting-place, he reached into his capacious memory and brought forth what I thought to be an even better tale.

THE DUMB WITNESS

Time was (said the Indian) when Ghulam Rasool, curling his beard and smearing his moustache, used to saunter through the Thieves' Bazaar, and expected everyone to bow low saying: *"Pahlawan sahib,* mighty wrestler, salutations to you."

It was, however, twenty years ago when the Grand Vizir appointed Rasool as Kotwal, at the head of the city police, for well did the Vizir know that the prize-fighter could wield the whip perfectly.

That day of which I speak, Ghulam Rasool's carriage escorted by his police body-servants came down the narrow dusty lane, and stopped outside the shop of Abdul Karim, the carpet-maker.

With much straining and creaking of the carriage springs, the Kotwal descended heavily and importantly, and was immediately besieged by a bunch of clamouring beggars, few of whom appeared to have more than the remotest link with mankind, grovelling in the dirt for the few coppers he threw among them.

"Akh! get out of my way," shouted Rasool, to yet another crowd of beggars who were fast approaching. The lash of his coachman's whip emphasised his master's words—for was not Rasool the police chief whose word was law?

And Karim, sitting cross-legged at his loom, had seen everything from the moment the carriage entered the bazaar, until it stopped, as he knew it would, in front of his own door.

He had also heard the cry of the beggars that "Allah might balance the scales in the favour of their patron." Mutely, too, did the carpet-maker join in that prayer: for it was a fervent petition that he might be delivered from hands out of which there seemed no escape. Still he did not raise his head from his work, until a shadow darkened the little doorway.

"Peace be upon you, Abdul."

"And upon you, too, Kotwal sahib of great name!" replied

the carpet-maker meekly.

"What is the condition of the bazaar?"

"Much labour for small return, master. The beardless English do not now buy like their fathers did—and bargain more, with half the knowledge."

The characteristic loud laugh of the visitor filled the stuffy little shop. Abdul knew that laugh and winced. Each of the previous laughters meant that he would have to make a carpet from which there would be no profit. Meant, too, that the work would have to be done at double the ordinary speed; worse luck, too, for it was the beginning of the season, and Abdul had to hawk his wares from door to door, from bungalow to bungalow, with little profit, for the sahibs had little money and less appreciation.

This and more raced through the mind of the carpet-maker as the Kotwal examined minutely the assortment of carpets which hung, as mute advertisements of profitably-spent hours.

"A . . . h!" The ejaculation caused Abdul to awaken from his reverie. He half turned as the other dragged out the finest rug in the shop, and threw it down with an aggressively defiant movement in front of Abdul.

"There, is not that a choice piece? Am I not one who knows?"

"Of a truth sahib, you know. Money pays but half for its value. The oil of my eyes has nearly dried making it!"

"What do you think I want? A linen *dhurri* at five rupees?"

"Nay, Kotwal sahib, well do I know your ability as a judge of carpets."

"Give ear to what I say," he commanded. "I want a rug four times the size of this!"

"Four times?" gasped the incredulous carpet-maker.

"Four times," came the reply. "It must be more alluringly worked than this. With a design of rosebuds in a garden of paradise and more, but in the same colours. It is for one who knows a creation from a mere bazaar piece!"

"It will cost many hundreds of rupees, sahib."

"Perhaps. But not to me surely, not to me?" The Kotwal's eyes narrowed.

Again the loud laugh rang out, filling the silence of Abdul's muteness.

"The time, too, is short," continued the client, "the work

must be completed in three months."

"That will mean all my work put aside. I shall not be able to carry my carpets round to sell. I am a poor man, Khan Kotwal, you know it. I cannot afford help."

"Yes," slowly replied the other meaningly, 'a poor man you may be, but a wise one!"

The carpet-maker's quick eyes darted to the visitor's swift gaze. Each understood the other perfectly.

"Moreover," continued the Khan, stressing each word, "The carpet is for no less a one than our judge, the learned Qadi himself!"

"The . . . Qadi?" stuttered Abdul.

"Yes. You and I like to be on good terms with the administrator of the law, brother. The Qadi can have men hanged!"

"Of a certainty," stuttered Abdul, without looking at his inquisitor, yet wincing under the implied lash in the words.

"The carpet will be ready then?"

A momentary hesitation followed, during which time Abdul became as yielding as a mesmerised rabbit.

"I will do my best, Kotwal sahib."

"Then I know the result will please even the Qadi," replied the Khan, slapping the miserable Abdul heavily on the shoulder. "Also I know you will be reasonable regarding the price, as you were before, very reasonable," he said stroking his beard.

"Luck is in your stars today, Abdul," called a neighbour, after the carriage had rumbled its way out of hearing. "Rich clients mean much profit."

"The return is small, brother."

"But how can it be when the Kotwal himself, who knows a carpet when he sees one, orders only the best?"

Abdul was silent, bending more closely over this work, and the neighbour went his way chuckling, as one does who knows he has touched a weak spot in another's defence.

"Profit! profit!" ejaculated Abdul, expectorating neatly on to a chosen spot out in the thoroughfare. "Profit is what a man has after his expenses are paid, while with the work I am forced to do for the Kotwal, I am but paid for the materials, and work for nothing."

"Four times the size!" ruminated Abdul, fingering the exquisite workmanship of the rug chosen by the Kotwal. "Even more elaborate! Ruin, that is what it will mean. Ruin! Coming upon me as surely as the day when the Earth will crumble into dust!"

"You and I like to be on good terms with the administrator of the law," the Kotwal had said.

"It was a bad business, that killing," thought the carpet-maker; and a worse, he kicked himself, to be discovered by the Kotwal. "Day and night have I toiled, and here am I, instead of being a fairly rich man, nothing but an afflicted one." Gloomily, vacantly, he gazed upon nothing in particular. But the news, which spreads as surely news can only travel in an Indian bazaar, had already caused the force, which musters against a man already stricken, to take the shape of a debtor at Abdul's door.

"That debt now you will be able to pay, O Abdul? Now the rich Kotwal has ordered so tasteful a rug, and has possibly paid something on account!"

"Give me time yet, brother, a little longer," pleaded Abdul.

With this unpleasant visitor gone, the carpet-maker fell to thinking. The carpet to be finished ought to be started at once. His wife was ill, and there was scarely any money to spare to pay the Hakim, the doctor who attended her.

"Am not I the unfortunate one, almost like unto the forgotten of Allah, and yet, so long as the hand of the Khan is over my head, like a falcon choosing the moment to swoop, I must, like its unfortunate prey, use my wit to escape it, but some day . . .

"The Qadi is a great and powerful man. It shows what the privilege of being independent can do for a man. Thirty years ago we were school-friends, taught by the same *Maulvi*. For years we remained friends, then our ways parted. I followed my father in the making of carpets; my friend chose the law.

"Then this killing and the power of the Khan came between us. The Khan who was ever jealous of our friendship, and the Khan had won!"

Some few minutes later Abdul, deep in the recollection of those early days, was laughing loudly at how he and the boy destined to become the Qadi had passed the hour after the midday meal, while the old teacher nodded over the effects of too much chicken pilau.

Being a simple man, Abdul kicked off his sandals, spread his rug, and turned his face towards Holy Mecca. The prayer over, as though to prove the efficacy of the orison, and even as he rose from his knees, an answer to the cry of his heart was vouchsafed to him. His mind cleared, his fear lifted.

The hour was late to begin a new piece of work, but the carpet-maker had found new hope, new courage. The finish of this carpet would mean, by the Mercy of Truth, the end of the thraldom of the Kotwal. Then catching sight of the pale, thin arch of the new moon he sobbed as he raised his hands, palms cupped upwards towards it.

As Abdul fastened the door of his shop, he paused awhile; and, throwing back his head, he laughed—a carefree laugh. For the first time in ten years freedom had made friends with him again.

From after the first prayer of the dawn, until long after the last prayer at night, Abdul sat cross-legged and toiled, bent almost double over the intricate pattern of the Qadi's carpet.

On feast days, when every good Moslem makes merry, Abdul worked on. Even the Kotwal who called to enquire about the progress of the work was moved to giving a few gold pieces on account.

Three months to a day the rug was finished. The Khan arrived with great show to examine the commission. For long his eyes gloated over it, from this angle and that, while Abdul watched him in breathless anxiety.

"It is a masterpiece, Abdul."

"One which perhaps only the Qadi and your good self can appreciate, master of the mighty police," said the carpet merchant.

"Indeed your words are those of truth, brother Abdul. I am even now on my way to visit the house beyond the Qadi's. Roll up the carpet and accompany us. As an extra appreciation, I will present you as the maker of this delight to the eye."

The Khan, with his back to the other, did not see the look which passed over Abdul's face at the invitation: or he might have regretted his proposal. Certain it is had he known what was passing through the mind of the carpet-maker he would have thought again about his offer. But the luck of Abdul was in, and he was going to hold on to it.

The two proceeded along the road to the Qadi's house, the Kotwal leading by a few paces as became his dignity. A casual observer might have thought, by the almost inspired expression on Abdul's face, that the carpet-maker was on the road leading directly to the wide open gates of the Sacred Garden.

The Qadi was at home. He received the Khan as one receives people who anticipate tangibly one's own hopes.

Abdul was duly presented, and spread the carpet out before the delighted eyes of the Qadi, who after examining it minutely for some minutes, turned to the Khan.

"This, Kotwal sahib, is exquisite. It will be my most valued piece. As you have another call to make, do so now, and return later, here. Meanwhile I will detain Abdul Karim, to discuss the mending of another valuable rug."

The eyes of the carpet-maker never left the face of the Qadi as the eyes of a man watches with concentrated attention those of another who holds his freedom or otherwise in his hands.

But Abdul learned nothing from the mobile face. Many a criminal had sat in the Qadi's court and lied his way to within the last gate leading to safety, thinking the calm, kind features of the quiet judge spoke of belief in his every word.

That last gate, however, was never destined to be unhasped, for between liberty and the miscreant was the final shock to be delivered.

Carefully the Qadi continued to examine the carpet. With feet spread wide apart, each hand resting heavily on a knee, the administrator of the law bent over, keenly intent upon the exquisite work of the centrepiece.

It seemed hours to Abdul before the other, straightening himself to his full six feet, faced him squarely and said: "Brother Abdul, I shall have speech with you in my own room."

Before the sentence was finished Abdul, vainly trying with a dry tongue to moisten dryer lips, followed the Qadi through the veranda into the Judge's private room. No word was spoken until seated on one side of a great table, and indicating a chair for his visitor on the other, the Qadi said:

"Tell me what is on your mind, Abdul Karim."

Abdul swallowed hard, he was aware of two piercing eyes

upon him, his trial had begun.

"Qadi Sahib, you stand for justice! I now appeal to you for it, after ten years of slavery."

The nod which the Qadi gave heartened Abdul.

"Ten years ago my eldest daughter was engaged to be married to the son of my brother, whom you know."

Again the Qadi nodded.

"Two days before the wedding she disappeared. Stolen! Stolen by Ghafur Sadiq, son of the silver merchant."

"Who was found dead a year later," interrupted the Qadi.

Abdul ignored the remark. He was reliving that time over again as he gripped the massive table for support.

"Months after, my daughter returned home alone, clad in rags, barefooted, her body starved and covered with bruises." Abdul struggled with his emotions, buried his face in his hands, and in an unsteady voice said:

"She came home . . . to die!"

"Days of fever and delirium followed, when she called upon Ghafur, begging him, praying that he might take her home. At other times her shrieks were terrible when, with arm raised as though shielding her face, she implored him to stop ill-using her.

"She died calling him to take her to her father for forgiveness, and that day I swore, upon my honour, to find him. For weeks, forgetful that I was earning nothing, that for many days I had not tasted food, that my clothes were dirty, even my prayers unsaid, I walked on and on from bazaar to bazaar, from village to village. I became mad, with one idea only in my mind, to track down the violator of my daughter and kill him. On and on I struggled in a world that contained only him and myself.

"One day while walking as one crazed on the outskirts of Peshawar, the frontier city where so many criminals strive to hide their guilt, I came upon him. He did not recognize me, my own brother would have passed me by, but I knew the scoundrel, would have known him in ten million million; I flung myself upon him, even my weakness left me and I bore him to the ground. My rage consumed me. My hands were about his throat, forcing, crushing, squeezing the loathesomeness out of him.

"'We have met at last, Ghafur Sadiq! It is I, Abdul Karim!

Yes, Abdul Kar . . . im!'

"How long I held him I do not know. It may have been for a day, or only an hour. My only fear was that I should let go too soon, and that he might come back to life.

"The sound of horses hooves brought me back to reality. Dropping his head, I rose to my feet to face the Khan, who until I told my name did not know me."

"'He is dead,' said the Khan.

"'I killed him,' I replied. 'An eye for an eye, a tooth for a tooth!'

"From that day, as the price of his silence, I have been obliged to make fine rugs for the Khan, without receiving anything for my work. Now greatly in debt, my life is scarcely worth living."

When Abdul had finished his story the eyes of the Qadi were still upon him. It was some minutes before he spoke.

"I have heard your story. My court is one of justice as well as law. To kill a man is a grave offence. Had you come to me years ago and told me what you have kept in your heart in secret, justice would have been done."

Abdul's eyes wandered upward to where, frescoed on the wall about the Qadi's seat, a blindfolded figure supported a giant pair of scales: above, in Persian calligraphy was the word: *Insaf*—justice.

The Qadi turned and fixed his eyes upon the same symbol.

"Justice has been done, my brother. You have avenged the death of your daughter, as well as having served a cruel 'sentence' for ten years. You have, I can assure you, made your last carpet for the Chief of the Police. From this day you are under the patronage of the Qadi, the administrator of justice. That is the finding of my court. Justice has been done. We must thank this carpet for its evidence, which has brought us together again. We shall meet often and talk over the old times. Let us begin tomorrow. Partake of your mid-day meal with me in comfort, old friend!"

If the monsoon rain soaked Abdul before he reached his little shop that night he was scarcely aware of it.

The following day the Kotwal drove into the bazaar as was his wont, and stopped outside the shop of Abdul Karim, the carpet-maker. That day the door of the shop was closed, nor did it open to the Khan's knocking. His heart missed several beats as his eyes lighted on the notice which seemed to glare back defiance at him. The notice which occupied the whole of Abdul Karim's window said:

"Under the patronage of the Qadi."

His heart would probably never have functioned properly again could he have seen the Qadi at that very moment, rocking with laughter, as the cunning Abdul related again how, as from a fold in his brain, a scheme to outwit the hated Kotwal had come to him. How he had set to work, weaving his petition into the centrepiece of the carpet, in the children's cypher which over thirty years ago he and the Qadi had concocted during the hours after the mid-day meal, while their respected white-bearded teacher slept off the effects of too much chicken and rice.

*　　*　　*

When the Indian had finished, the Muezzin, who hailed from the same Afghan glens as I, rose to speak, with a strange expression on his face.

"The indications which come to man through unexpected sources are well portrayed in this tale. It could be taken as symbolical of that Hand and Mind which is ever communicating, while we, unless made aware of it, seldom pause to listen for its silent words, or to look for its handiwork, pointing to events in our lives. In order to emphasis this, I will now tell you something, in the most direct way, of how, when in Turkish exile and planning to return home, I was subject to such an intervention."

After such a tantalising introduction, the pilgrims clamoured for the "entire story, omitting no detail", and the old man started his story with a strange experience in Istanbul.

THE WARNING

It was in the bazaars of this Gateway of the East one evening that I underwent an experience which perhaps more than any other made me realise that occult practice is much more in vogue, much more an everyday thing, whether in the East or the West, than some people might imagine. I was wandering down one of the long winding streets or lanes of that crowded city, when I felt someone grasp my arm. Aware of the dangers which beset the stranger in the city of the Golden Horn, I shook off the hand which detained me, but had only continued a few yards when I felt its grasp once more. Turning angrily I beheld a little old man with a grey beard and turbaned head, perhaps as insignificant a being as East or West could show.

"Be off," I said impatiently, "I have nothing to give you."

"But, Effendi," he replied, "I have something to give *you*—good advice."

Slightly amused, because he appeared to be a character, I resolved to humour him.

"Good advice is always welcome to a good man," I said sententiously, "and I will listen to yours with pleasure."

"Come with me then," he said, and began to draw me by the sleeve towards a low doorway. Now this was wholly another matter. As I have said, Stambul can be a dangerous place, and I was taking no risks.

"Have no fear," he whispered, and something in his voice reassured me. I passed through the doorway, then through the lobby into one of the oddest apartments I have ever seen. It was hung with pale yellow silk, behind which lamps were burning, and its only furniture was a metal table which stood in the middle of this small apartment, and two heaps of cushions.

Towards one of these the ancient waved me and then seated himself on the other. The lamps at once automatically lowered to a dim glow. Neither of us spoke a word. We just waited.

Suddenly, I know not how, I saw a man's shape standing by

the table. How he came to be in the room I cannot say. I could just observe his outline, tall and spare.

"You intended to go to Afghanistan?" said a deep voice.

"That is my intention," I replied wonderingly, "but who are you, and why do you ask?"

"My identity does not matter," said the voice, "but you must not go to your native land. There will be broils and tumults there, civil war and shedding of blood, and if you, a nobleman, are recognized, you will assuredly come to an evil end."

Now at this time Amanullah the King was in Italy, and all was well within his kingdom. Indeed, it looked as though he had a long lease of power, so I laughed aloud at the warning.

As if my laugh had broken some spell, the lamps went up—but no figure was revealed standing by the iron table. I jumped up from my pile of cushions, and confronted the old man as he rose from his.

"What is the meaning of this farce?" I asked angrily. "Do you think you can impress me by your trickeries?"

He shrugged his shoulders. "It is no trickery," he said simply. "You have been given good advice. Be wise and take it."

Thinking that it might be a diplomatic dodge to keep me out of Afghanistan at a crisis, and that I might incur some risk by lingering here, I hurried away. But the effect of the incident remained. Something much more powerful than fear restrained my homeward progress, and I resolved to go to Anatolia and await events. But nothing happened. After remaining there some months I went elsewhere, and in due course resumed my journey in other parts of the East.

Many months passed, and I had almost forgotten the incident, when news arrived of the rebellion in Afghanistan. I was sitting, of all places, in New Street restaurant in Baghdad enjoying a cup of coffee after lunch, looking dreamily out of the window and pondering over the affairs of my country, when suddenly I saw among the crowd the face of the old man whom I had met in Constantinople, bearded and turbaned. For an instant it hovered before me, with a look of supreme intelligence, then it was gone as quickly as it had come. It did not vanish. It simply was not there. In vain I peered down the length of the street: no further glimpse did I obtain of it.

Now what in the name of all that is mysterious is a man to make of this? Were it merely a diplomatic stratagem, am I to assume that I was of sufficient importance in the affairs of Afghanistan that such a move was rendered necessary? Who would have been behind it?

I am rather inclined to think that we humans and our careers are of much more importance in the eyes of Providence than the rise or fall of kingdoms, and that peculiar and mysterious agencies surround us for the purpose of protecting us and warning us regarding circumstances which might easily cut short our lives and destroy the train of thought which bears us, as on the water of a stream, to the higher regions of soul-existence. I have heard and read of many such incidents as that I have related which would seem, in the aggregate, to bear out this theory. Certain persons may either be of particular value to Providence, or their spiritual condition may be in such a state at a given time that great injury might be done to the human soul were the body subjected to danger. I fully believe that the supernatural plays a much greater part in our existences than we actually know.

Scoffers may say that I dreamed or imagined the face of the old man in Baghdad. I can only state in reply to this that I saw him as clearly as I did the other people in the thoroughfare at the time. It was no wraith-like apparition, but a face of flesh and blood.

Some day I hope to return to Stambul and stand face to face with him once more. But I question if he will be there. I rather think that he will be about his Master's business elsewhere. Indeed, both in East and West, I have encountered other people whom I have enough evidence to suspect were also engaged in that business, agents of powers mysterious whose precise vocation most blinded mortals can scarcely comprehend.

How little do we know of the world after all. New marvels of nature are almost daily unrolled to our view. But surely the marvels of man and of the human soul are vastly more amazing and terrifying. Sometimes they seem to bulk so largely to me, to invade my days with such insistence, that they appear far more imminent and important than anything else. And the small glimpses of those mysteries which have been vouchsafed to me lead me to entertain more than a suspicion that they may actually be our chief business in life—a business more enthralling and enormously more important than any of those more human and conventional avocations on which we lavish our time with such thoughtlessness and carelessness of the loftier side of our natures.

* * *

From Syria, we made our way through Lebanon and then hastened to the first goal of our caravan: Jerusalem, where the rigours of the road were as much forgotten as the entertainment of the tales which we had heard, to be replaced by the emotional pull of piety and the religious feelings which, at a certain level, affect all human beings.

JERUSALEM THE HOLY

To me, as a Moslem, the City of Jerusalem ranks second in sanctity only to Mecca. The people of my faith, after performing their religious ceremonies at Mecca, year by year make if they can pilgrimages to the Holy City of Jerusalem. According to our belief, the Prophet Mohamed the Messenger "flew on his white steed to meet God," from a red stone of this city. That slab is entombed here in the Dome of the Rock. And here, too, one of our great prophets, Jesus, preached. His mother, Mary, too, has great reverence shown to her in our beliefs. It is, therefore, sacrilegious in the eyes of Islam to term Jerusalem anything but holy. When I trekked to that Sacred City this spirit filled my mind.

As I drew nearer and nearer Jerusalem, a mingled feeling of joy and respect came upon me. The passing crowd, a living, pulsating pageant of early religion, and the Holy Dome of the Rock framed in a sycamore avenue spoke of a different epoch.

Giant bells were tolling somewhere, but their music struck upon my ears in no material tone. "So this is Al-Quds!— Jerusalem, the Holy" I said, "of which Allah Himself speaks in His Book"; and lifted my hands in a prayer of thanksgiving, for had the Prophet of Mecca not made his night-journey from Jerusalem to the Celestial Throne, and the dead here risen to life at the Messiah's bidding?

There was a nip in the sunlit air of the city as I walked from shrine to shrine, during that Christmas week, negotiating its narrow bazaars, swarming with nationals of all countries from Poland to Java.

"*Sabahal Khair!* May thy morning be peaceful!" shouted a Christian pilgrim guide to a Moslem shopkeeper, but his reply wishing the same felicity was drowned by the high-toned inquiry of one of the party about an Arab silk gown that hung in the shop. That lady pilgrim would not pay twenty dollars for it. She could buy the same kind cheaper in New York, she said.

Hurriedly they passed on, scarcely noticing the Fifth Station of the Cross. But I lingered on, meditating about the agony of Jesus down the stone-paved Via Dolorosa. What history has that route of arches not made for man, and yet the donkey-driver unconcernedly sold water down the lane and the Jewish priests with their curled love-locks walked past the scenes on which Europe's civilization is built.

Through the arcaded bazaars where you can purchase anything from an ancient Damascus blade to a fashionable necktie, passed Christian, Jew and Moslem, dressed almost alike in the long flowing garb of the Arab; only a few modernised Arabs wear European dress. Here and there a Greek priest with tall black hat, or a Jew with a rimmed fur cap, glides mysteriously round the corner; or again Moslem divines with their flapping coats reaching down to their ankles wearing be-turbaned fezzes, hurry on to the Mosque of Omar. Ponies, sheep and goats jostle with the crowd: but the camel ignoring humanity makes his own way, or stops to nibble at the carrots at a vegetable shop. Beyond lies the Church of the Holy Sepulchre, grim and steeped in the holiness of ages.

It is impossible not to be impressed by the sight of Christendom's most holy place; and after buying a few wax tapers from a shop before entering the precincts, I observed that it was a Moslem doorkeeper who kept the gate of this church as an hereditary privilege since the time of Khalifa Omar, Companion of the Prophet.

Along one side of the wall of the court sat beggars chanting; and a few blind men, too, had gathered there, who believing in the curative value of the "pilgrims' breaths," solicited that breath as every devotee emerged from the church. Thus they hoped to regain their sight. Small Arab boys tried to sell to me sacred pictures from Hebron, glass bracelets and toys made of olive wood.

Immediately inside the church, the pilgrims bowed low, many kissed the Stone of Anointing, then, respectfully, they passed on. In the Rotunda square pillars support a dome—which having been damaged by the earthquake, was then under repair—and although the interior might be a disappointment as compared with what one sees in European cathredrals, it is not exactly masonry that is of consequence.

The spirit of the place mattered to me. Upon one of the galleries they were chanting so beautifully that the accompaniment of a musical instrument would have killed its soul. Swarthy Egyptian Christians clad in their native costume sang so emotionally before the Sepulchre in Arabic, that I felt how strange it is to regard Jesus as the white man's Christ.

The sepulchre where Jesus was laid, although no more than twenty-four feet long, fifteen feet wide and not very high, appeared to me a mighty thing. The heart of a great religion lay there. But entering the marble antechamber, and stooping under a four-feet high doorway, so that one stood in the Chapel of the Holy Sepulchre itself, sensations rose in my mind which made me realize how great the influence of a feeling of Sacredness can be. A Greek monk stood motionless and mute, watching a peasant youth who had placed his rosary upon the rock-hewn Sepulchre. Tears rolled down the boy's cheeks as he knelt beside the tomb.

Outside again I counted eighty people going in and out, in less than ten minutes. The shrine was never empty. But judging by their dresses, the pilgrims appeared poor. Had wealth, I wondered, kept the rich away from this cradle of Christianity?

Wrapped in the atmosphere of these experiences, I zigzagged my way down the street, and saw the most impressive sight of all when old men and young knelt in prayer at a Station of the Cross, whilst Moslem guards led a procession of Franciscan Fathers through the crowded bazaars. This practice of the Moslem guards leading a Christian procession is but another survival of the time of Khalifa Omar's entry into Jerusalem in 637. He not only gave liberty of worship to Christians, but actually made his coreligionists responsible for the safety of the Christians and their Churches.

Walking past a narrow lane I came upon the Church of St. Anne, close to which is the Pool of Bethesda. A White Father explained about its discovery in 1871, and conversed with me in my native Farsee. Beyond it is the reputed grave of Bibi Maryam, the Mother of Jesus, whose memory is also sacred to the Moslems. And further on are those peaceful-looking olive trees in the Garden of Gethsemane, the twisted trunks of which could now tell me little of Christ's great agony.

Wandering round the city I came upon the Jews' Wailing

Place. Superficially it is nothing but a block of stones some
fifteen feet long to about five feet high, the celebrated western
wall of the Temple; but spiritually it seems to have a deep
significance to those who cling to it more fondly than a mother
clings to an only child. It was Friday. White-bearded men,
shaven youths, women and children, wept against the stones. A
woman cried so bitterly that in another moment I could have
joined her. Some of the mourners bought holy oil from a man
nearby and lit tiny earthen lamps in the broken places of the
wall. His eyes, too, had a sad look, and in between his busy
moments of selling oil, he helped a few old men to say their
prayers.

Just behind the Moslem quarter, I entered the Noble
Sanctuary of the Dome, under which lies a large slab of rock
from where the Prophet Mohamed is believed to have journeyed heavenwards one particular night, and thus rendered it
holy to the Moslems. This vast courtyard has seven gates. Since
Kalif Abdul Malik built the dome of this edifice and the Sultan
Salahuddin, 'Saladin', restored it, the shrine of the Red Rock
has seen pilgrims from every part of the globe. I reached the
building by eight flights of steps. Porticoes stand gracefully in
indescribable glory at the top of each. Coloured tiles cover the
octagonal sides and and the cupola rises to one hundred and
eight feet. Verses from the Holy Koran are inscribed in Arabic
upon it. Simplicity is blended with magnificence around the
Red Rock inside, chandeliers and lamps that hang in the arches
are but material signs of devotion, and the pious history of my
faith hovers on that mass of solid rock, apparent only to the eyes
of the faithful.

There is nothing like it in the world to a Moslem, unless it be
the Shrine of Mecca. The intense silence moved me to tears, the
message of the Prophet I felt forcibly, all else was void. In the
heart of that stone was buried annals of more than a thousand
years.

The Mosque of Al Aksa facing the Dome has charms and
sanctity of its own, because by praying in it Moslems may
acquire much merit: and the Koran speaks of it frequently.
Dreamy-eyed Uzbek pilgrims from Bokhara lingered there
with their Arab brothers of the Islamic fraternity. Others of the
same beliefs from India were just as much at home. Geographi-

cal disparity of our home lands we did not feel, as we stood facing towards Mecca when the Muezzin called the prayers. The same bending and swaying, the same chanting and mutely lifting upturned palms we engaged in as we would anywhere else. A Moslem has really no nationality other than his religion. We could not understand each other's language. Yet as Moslem pilgrims we were of one fold, one patron, one ideal, in that sacred city. Then they showed me the site where the Moslem pilgrims walked in procession, holding banners and displaying active manifestations of festivity to Nebi Musa.

In meditation and prayer, day passed day in Jerusalem, until the Christian pilgrim tourists filled the town. But the idea of "doing pilgrimage" of some of them did not appeal to me, and while this rush was on, I journeyed to Jericho to avoid it. Returning to the Holy City on the Christmas Day, I walked to Bethlehem. A thin rain was falling but I walked on. To ride to the birthplace of Jesus was to deprive myself of the spirituality of the occasion; and truly marvellous was the spectacle of the procession going through the streets to the Church of Nativity. The deep devotional air was unmistakable. As I trekked back to Jerusalem some monks were also marching back with their orphan wards.

Standing just near the Chapel of the Ascension on the Mount of Olives, I noticed how true it is to call Jerusalem "a city on a hill." From that spot I could see the panorama of religions entombed in their buildings. A plateau rose in front of me from right to left marking the Haram Sharif, the Dome of the Rock, towering above its surroundings. Beyond that, blocks of houses forming David Street carried the gaze as far as the tower of the Church of the Holy Sepulchre. The building Notre Dame de France lay at the furthest end. Past it, a road like a white ribbon stretched away to Jaffa. And peering down through the branches of olive trees on to the valley below where the religious dramas of man have so often been enacted, I noticed the atmosphere of peacefulness that now hovered over it all. These were not only buildings, stones, brick and mortar; rather each was a book to me; and when I saw a woman carrying a conical shaped earthern water vessel on her head to her husband who was ploughing the fields in the olive grove, how well she fitted into the picture, I thought, of this restful scene.

Immersed in these thoughts, I must have sat long there under an olive tree, for the sun's rays were already paling upon the minarets, and bells had begun to toll from a dozen churches, whilst the Moslem muezzins called the faithful to prayer. It was, indeed, a struggle to tear oneself away from the scenes of that spiritual detachment to the tawdry glamour of modern life. This pilgrimage had left a deep impression upon my mind, and sitting later amongst the hurly-burly of the superficial existence of town life in Europe, I did not need to close my eyes to see the moving-picture film of the Noble City with her great drama writ large upon her face. That shall ever stand out in my memory.

In the Second Holiest Place of Islam

It is truly said that one half of the world knows nothing of what the other half is doing, for despite the fact that an event of an international character happened when the Jordanian King opened the second holiest place in Islam in Jerusalem, little or nothing about this important event seems to have been conveyed to the West. In order to appreciate its significance, a few points have to be mentioned here. The City of Jerusalem ranks as the holiest place of Islam only after Mecca. The Muslims prayed towards it before they were recommended to direct their prayers Kaaba-wards, for in the heart of this Sacred City lies the Haram Sharif, where the Rock and the Aksa Mosque are situated. Again and again the Koran mentions the holiness of these two places, so that many pilgrims, after they have been to Mecca, trek to Jerusalem to bend low to these shrines, permeated as they are with the Islamic traditions of centuries. Now, these sanctified buildings were greatly damaged; the Mosque of Aksa especially was in peril of a complete collapse. The general deterioration, which besets all buildings, coupled with a lack of regular repairs before the First World War and finally an earthquake that shook Jerusalem, made it imperative that the Supreme Muslim authorities, under the guidance of the Grand Mufti of Jerusalem, attended to the restoration of the Mosque immediately.

It was found that the Dome of the Aksa was leaning to one

side to the extent of about thirty-five meters. First of all the German architects who built the beautiful railway station at Hyder Pasha in Istanbul, were invited to undertake the task; but they refused to handle it, thinking it beyond their skill, and ultimately Kamal Bey, a Turkish architect, with the help of two Arabs working for six years, accomplished the restoration.

Practically all labour employed was Palestinian, as also the material. Close to the Haram Sharif, I had often seen Arab boys and their elders hard at work in connection with their many crafts for the restoration of the Mosque. They worked with an earnestness almost approaching religious fervour; they sang sacred verses as they worked. In a large airy room hundreds of them were busy, some cutting the marble slabs, others drawing and working beautiful floral designs or Koranic inscriptions on stone. Further on I saw sheets of copper with gold leaf being hammered into patterns to be put on the wooden pillars; but nothing interested me more than the example of the pure Arab art as, working deftly with small knives, they cut floral designs in a cement slab in a sort of delicate lace-work, on the reverse of which they studded pieces of coloured glass. These were the windows of the Mosque, and when they were placed high up in their positions, in the half-light of the interior of the building, the effect was remarkably beautiful. They appeared to me to be like the fine marble filigree work of the Taj Mahal at Agra, with the final effect of a stained glass window.

Neither the beauty of this, nor that of the Dome of the Rock, can be appreciated to the full if you do not visit every nook and corner of the whole area of about ninety acres which comprises the Haram Sharif, wherein these shrines are situated. To do this, you must enter by the way of the Cotton Merchants' Bazaar. The whole strikes you as an enchanted dreamland, a plateau on which towers the mighty Dome: arches are seen here and there, cypress trees peep out between the buildings and minarets, the long-robed and beturbaned holy men move about in all solemnity, the faithful are hurrying to the mosque, others bending low in silent meditation, and all is quiet, awe-inspiring, a world of its own. Presently a Muezzin mounts the minaret at the end of the esplanade and calls the faithful to prayer, his chant taken up by another. "God is Great, God is

Great . . ." they repeat in the four corners of the vast space, and worshippers swell the ranks in the noble sanctuary of Aksa. A thousand voices are hushed to silence, only the Imam recites passages from the Koran to the end of the service. Then they emerge from the Mosque and enter the Dome for meditation, or sit mutely telling the beads of their rosaries in the low-roofed rooms around the plateau of the Rock.

Solomon erected his Temple here, till the Chaldæans destroyed it. Seventy years after that it was rebuilt, only to be destroyed again; but Herod repaired it and gave it to the Jews, during whose occupancy Jesus, being of the tribe of Judah, could not enter it further than other Jews. In the court of that Temple, too, the infant Christ was presented by his Mother, and ultimately from that place, according to the Moslem belief, the Prophet Mohammed made his night's journey to the Throne of Allah. The Caliph Abdul Malik caused this Dome to be built over the rock, but the original was destroyed by an earthquake and rebuilt in A.D. 1022, but for its later glories the name of Sultan Salahuddin is prominently mentioned.

One climbs eight flights of steps to reach the esplanade, passing through a beautiful portico step on the plateau. On the Day of Judgment, so Moslem belief has it, the scales to weigh human actions will be suspended from these porticoes of the Dome of the Rock. The octagonal building, about 180 feet in diameter, is surmounted by a huge cupola of nearly eighty feet. First of all one steps onto a marble slab to enter. Its interior beggars description. Rays coloured by the stained glass of the windows penetrate the half-lighted interior. In passing, the light makes the gorgeous gold-work glitter in the lining of the Dome, and the whole play of colour blends with the grey-brown colour of the Rock. It strikes one mute with wonderment. What history lies buried in the heart of that piece of stone? That under it lies the Ark of Noah, that the roaring waters which have no depths are below it, that it has the impress of the hand of Angel Gabriel, who stayed the rock, are all beliefs among the Moslems.

Close to it is the Mosque of Aksa, which Christian writers assert has the appearance of a basilica, and was founded in 536 by Justinian in honour of the Blessed Virgin; but all authentic record is against this, for even Ferguson admits the Muslim view that it was built by Caliph Abdul Malik in place of what remained of its former wooden structure. As you enter it, you cannot help being struck by the purposeful erection of its nave and aisles. It is curious in the sense that it seems a combination of various architectures round which the Arab conception of a sacred edifice is evolved. Some capitals, for instance, show forms of the acanthus leaf, the arches are wider, but its connecting beams are definitely Arab.

Saladin's restoration is marked by an inscription dated 1186, and the decoration of the Dome is unlike that of the Dome of the Rock. Prayer niches flanked by marble are unique in their beauty and craftmanship. The pulpit is of wood, wood of the cedars of Lebanon which Salahuddin imported; and from its skilful execution one does not wonder to hear that the craftsman who made it was honoured by being raised to the highest office of the realm. This sort of work I saw done in ivory and mother-of-pearl on wood carving in the villages near Adana in Turkey as well, but nothing of it reaches the excellence of the pulpit in the Aksa Mosque.

In every quarter of the Haram there is always some place to hold your interest. Solomon's stables under this mosque are the subject of wonderment still; there is, too, the place marked as the resting-place of the murderers of Thomas à Becket; whilst another spot is pointed out as the Throne of Solomon: and what of the Gateway of the Chain from which, it is believed, a chain ascends to high heaven, but is visible, it is said, only to the spiritually gifted? Every corner of this plateau has its traditions and a place in the hearts of men which cannot be effaced. It is sanctified with holiness only second to Mecca, in the estimation of the one-fifth of the human race owing allegiance to Islam.

*   *   *

When we entered the burning deserts of the Hejaz, in the Arabian Peninsula where Mecca is situated, we still had many days' travel before us. With us were two Imams, the men who lead the Faithful in prayer, and I was enthralled to hear emerge, during a discussion between them, an unusual version of a tale which surely must have been told among the peoples of the East almost since time began.

This is none other than the recital of the Pulse of the Princess. . .

THE PULSE OF THE PRINCESS BANOU

"Piety," said the first Imam, "does not always bring pleasure in its train, else would our serene Sultan be the most happy of men."

"You say truly," replied the second Imam, "for who can doubt that the Sultan Sunjar is a just and upright prince. Yet he is doleful, and since he made the journey to the shrine of the Master Khaja Bahauddin in Bukhara, he has surely been the saddest among the rulers of the earth."

"It was not always so," said the first Imam. "We can remember when the court was blithe enough and when music and festivity reigned within its walls from morning till night. They say that the Sultan is sad because the Princess Banou, his only daughter, suffers from an unknown and maybe incurable malady."

And so it was most surely. Some strange sickness which could not be defined had seized upon the princess. Her face, only the most beautiful in the world, had grown thin and grey, her eyes had lost their lustre; her brow, once smooth as an unruffled lake, was furrowed with lines of care. Many hakims, physicians from many countries, had tried to cure the princess of her malady, but all had failed. The ailment from which she suffered seemed beyond the wisdom of the physicians to cure. And Sultan Sunjar, as his daughter drooped as a fading lily on its stalk, grew more harsh and tyrannical every day. So often had he been disappointed by the quacks who swarmed to the court to try to cure the Princess Banou, that he swore a great oath that any who now sought to do so must take his life in his hand. To him who succeeded in freeing the princess from the malady which was gradually destroying her, he promised anything he should ask, even to half his kingdom. But, did he fail to perform a cure, he would be put to death, and his head would be placed on a spear above the gate of the city.

Now, at the time when this story begins, the city gate had as

115

many heads rotting on its summit as there were bricks in its fabric, so that strangers arriving at the place and seeing the hakims' turbans from a distance thought that a great meeting of physicians was being held on the broad roof of the gate. And the princess grew weaker each day.

But one morning a stranger, rather shabbily attired, landed at the port of the city, a little aged-seeming man with white elf-locks and bent shoulders, wrapped up in a great robe of faded green. His pointed nose and slant eyes gave him somewhat the appearance of a ferret, and men naturally avoided him. He called himself Shadrach the Physician, and requested an immediate audience of the Sultan.

It chanced that the Sultan was in anything but a placid frame of mind that morning, and when it was announced to him that one calling himself Shadrach the Physician desired audience of him, he roared like a lion in wrath.

"Another of those empirics!" he cried. "Well, bring the wretch before me. But if he cannot cure my daughter, and that almost immediately, give him to know that his head will join the others above the city gate."

So Shadrach was admitted. He made low obeisance, but showed no sign of fear when the Sultan assured him of speedy death did he fail in his intention.

"My head, O pillar of the universe," he said meekly, 'sits very securely on my shoulders, and unless I greatly err it shall remain there. May I behold the princess?"

The Princess Banou was brought to him. She seemed pale as ivory as she disposed herself on the steps of her father's throne which were covered with the choicest carpets of Isfahan. The hakim might not address the princess, but seating himself beside her, he held her wrist between his thumb and his finger to take the beat of her pulse. And then to the amazement of the Sultan and all his court, he began to tell her stories. At first, he told her tales of the lives of kings and sultans, stories of adventure by land and sea, of battles, and of kingdoms lost and won.

But, as he proceeded, never once did the pulse of the princess flicker or betray the least emotion on her part. Then, the hakim told her most surprising tales, of hidden treasure, of caves in which bandits had secreted their ill-gotten gains, of jewels buried with dead queens and recovered again after generations of searching, yet never the slightest tremor he felt in the pulse he so carefully tested. The river of blood in the heart-vein flowed on slowly from the absence of its rain.

Then he spoke of his travels. He told her of his sojourn in all the adjacent lands—in India, Persia, Arabia. Still the pulse ran smoothly. But when he spoke of Bukhara which the princess had lately visited in the company of her father, her pulse gave a great leap, and a thin mantling of pink suffused her pale cheeks.

"Ha," thought the hakim. "So the mention of Bukhara agitates her?"

So he continued to harp upon Bukhara, of its mosques, its bazaars, its palaces, its streets, one by one; but it was not until he came to the bazaar of the jewellers in his survey of the city, that the pulse of the princess leapt once again.

"So," thought the hakim, "we grow ever warmer. The cause of the malady of this young woman, it would seem, must be sought in the bazaar of the jewellers."

So the hakim pursued his theme, and knowing Bukhara and everyone of importance therein very intimately, he began to describe the shop of every jeweller in the bazaar. And when at last he came to the name of Aboul Fazil, one of the youngest and handsomest jewellers in the bazaar, the princess started, trembled exceedingly, and well-nigh fainted. Yet she spoke no word, for royal etiquette did not permit a princess to address a mere hakim.

The hakim respectfully signed to the Sultan to dismiss his daughter, and when she had retired, he said: "O pillar of the universe, the case is clear. Your daughter, the princess, is pining for love of Aboul Fazil, the handsomest young jeweller in the bazaar of precious stones in Bukhara!"

Now the Sultan, although he was amazed at the skill of Shadrach, was angry when he heard that his daughter had fallen in love with a mere jeweller, but he cherished her so greatly that, in order to save her life, he would have married her to a wandering fakir. So he immediately dispatched messengers to Aboul Fazil, entreating him to come to his capital without delay.

And in due time the young man arrived in the city. He was tall and strikingly handsome and attired like a prince. And from the moment the Princess beheld him and spoke with him, she at once began to grow better, so that in the course of a few days she had quite recovered and appeared to enjoy the most radiant health. And Aboul Fazil was treated like a prince, honours were heaped upon him and he was lodged in a suite of the royal chambers.

Great was the satisfaction of the Sultan, and in his gratitude to the hakim he enquired of him the nature of his reward. But Shadrach, in his modesty, refused all wealth and honours, merely requesting to be made grand vizier of the kingdom. When he heard this request the Sultan was dumbfounded. Great wrath arose within him, but he had pledged his word, and seeing that Shadrach was indeed a shrewd fellow, he agreed to the suggestion with the best grace he could muster.

In no great time, however, it became clear that the jeweller, Aboul Fazil, as is the way with such people, had quite lost his head owing to the dignities and attentions which had been so profusely bestowed upon him. Dressed in the choicest silks and smothered in jewels, he strutted to and fro through the palace like a peacock. Even to the highest dignitaries of the court he assumed an attitude of insufferable rudeness, and to the Sultan himself he was curt and overbearing. With the Princess he was masterful and disdainful. He insisted that, when their nuptials were celebrated, he should be recognized as heir to the throne, and that the government of the largest province should be placed in his hands.

In great displeasure and disappointment the Sultan sought counsel of the hakim.

"My daughter's happiness is everything to me," he cried, "yet this wretch whom I have taken to my bosom, and whom I have treated like my own son born, offends my court with his riotous insolence and effrontery. What do you advise?"

"O illustrious one," said Shadrach, "there is only one course of action open to us. We must wean the Princess Banou from her affection for this orgulous and offensive person, and send him back to his booth in Bukhara."

"Easier said than done," shouted the Sultan. "She is besotted with the creature. If we remove him she will droop as before, and will almost certainly perish. All that he does seems to her perfectly natural and even highly amusing, so blind is her worship of him. Only yesterday when I called for sherbet cooled with snow, this son of Eblis verily snatched the cup out of the slave's hands and quaffed its gratefulness to the dregs, and she, bewitched as she is, laughed aloud. He should be lashed on the soles of his feet with the koorbash."

"I sincerely sympathize with your Majesty," replied Shadrach soothingly, "but we will gain nothing by harsh measures—indeed, the very reverse. No, let us call craft to our aid—craft which has overthrown men a thousand times more handsome and more cunning than this Aboul Fazil."

Now the Sultan greatly trusted the shrewdness of the hakim, so he left the matter entirely in his hands. And Shadrach gave out that he must go on a journey and would be away for several weeks. And attiring himself in his old robes of a wandering physician, he took a horse from the Sultan's stables and rode southwards. And he passed through Khorasan, and by Isfahan, and Luristan, and by Baghdad, he crossed the Syrian desert, and Arabia Petræa, and came at last to Egypt.

Arrived in the Nileland, he rode to the Pyramid of Hawara in the Fayyoum, where the great Labyrinth of Egypt is situated, which it took the reigns of twelve kings to build. The entrance was of white marble, and the interior contained thirty separate regions, each of which with its vast palace, the whole excavated out of the living rock and situated underground.

And by some art of which he had knowledge, Shadrach traversed the labyrinthine galleries, making his way in the thick darkness by the light of a small lamp only; past porticoes and banqueting halls, and the statues of gods and kings which littered the length and breadth of this city beneath the earth. And in some of the palaces there were doors which, when he opened them as he passed, emitted a terrible sound like the reverberations of thunder. And here and there lay the mummies of sacred crocodiles.

But none of these things frightened Shadrach. Carefully counting his steps, he walked slowly through the heavy gloom, until he had taken seven hundred and seventy-seven steps. Then he halted, and turning slowly to his left, traversed seventy-seven more steps. And now before him was a lofty pylon, in which was a door of two pieces, very high, and cast in bronze.

119

And on this door he knocked in a certain manner, and after some delay, the door opened slowly on its hinges, disclosing a thin shaft of light far within. Shadrach entered fearlessly, advancing straightway into an inner chamber, where a light burned high in the roof, and on a couch an old man, so wizened that he looked like a monkey, lay looking scarce alive.

"Hail, father of all wisdom," cried the hakim, prostrating himself before the withered ancient. "I have travelled all the way from the country of the Sultan Sunjar to take counsel of you."

"And what," said the sage, "brings Shadrach the Physician to Egypt?" Then Shadrach acquainted him with the manner in which affairs stood at the court, and proceeded to ask a boon.

"What I desire," he said, "is to procure a drug which, if taken by a young and handsome person, will make him look old and ugly, but which, if it is taken by an old and ill-favoured person, will render him young and handsome."

The ancient pondered the request for some time. Then he spoke. "Such a potion is to be had," he said, "but it is difficult to prepare. Indeed, there is one rare substance indispensable to its making, and that is the blood of a man who is over a hundred years of age, for the blood of such a man contains both the virtues of youth, because he has lived so long, and the venomous qualities of great age, for the same reason."

The hakim looked long and meaningly at the ancient. "You have more than a hundred years, O father of wisdom," he said gently. "Would not some of your blood suffice?"

The old man seemed terrified. He looked at Shadrach in great fear, trembling exceedingly, but said naught.

"Come, how much blood is essential for this experiment?" asked the hakim brutally.

"As much as will fill the palm of one hand," whispered the sage, "and I fear there is not so much in my whole body."

"Now as I am a physician," cried Shadrach, "I can assuredly draw such a small supply of blood from you without mishap." And taking a knife and cup from his scrip, he bent down and opened a vein in the old man's arm. The blood ran so slowly that he feared there would not be enough. So he squeezed the arm, whereat the ancient man called out shrilly; but eventually as much as would fill a man's palm oozed from the wound.

Then he bound up the wound, and bade the sage prepare the potion, while he rested and refreshed himself. He ate of the millet cakes in his pocket, and then, casting himself down on the bed where the ancient had lain, fell fast asleep.

And so weary was he with his long journey that he slept for two days without wakening. And on the morning of the third day, when he opened his eyes, he found the ancient standing over him, with two phials in his hands. One was of red colour, the other of a sickly green hue.

"Here are the potions," said the sage. "You must exercise great care in their use. Each day you must put three drops of either liquid into the food or drink of the person whom you wish to transform, no more and no less. The red potion will bestow youth upon an old man, and that which is of a green colour will make a young man old—but only by degrees. Shadrach, this I would not have done for you had you not been of the same secret brotherhood as myself, for you have shown no mercy to an old man."

"Come, father, be reasonable," said Shadrach laughing. "Where should I have found another man over a hundred years old?" And ignoring the chattering protests of the ancient, he carefully wrapped up the phials in his scrip, and making his way out of the labyrinth, went in search of his horse.

He found the beast in a field of millet near the river, where it had done great havoc to the crop, and, mounting it, rode off. For many days he rode, until at last he came once more, very weary, to the court of the Sultan Sunjar.

By this time, matters were at their worst. The wedding of Aboul Fazil and the princess had been arranged to take place within seven days, and even now the graceless wretch was actually sitting on the Sultan's throne, issuing ukases and commands, and generally oppressing everyone. But the Sultan was glad to see Shadrach, who assured him that soon all would be well.

And so the cunning hakim sought the kitchen and gave orders to the chief cook that all dishes intended for Aboul Fazil must first be inspected by himself, as the royal bridegroom had so ordered it. And every day at the noontide meal he poured three drops from the green phial into Aboul Fazil's food.

On the first day the handsome young jeweller complained of feeling very fatigued, and vented his displeasure on everyone. On the second day great pouches gathered beneath his eyes, and he seemed worn and haggard. On the third day his hair, which was dark and abundant, began to show patches of grey, and he stooped badly, and stumbled in his walk. On the fourth day his face was as the face of an old man.

Meanwhile the hakim had been careful to take the contents of the red phial. On the first day he felt and looked stronger. On the second, his face seemed more youthful, and his cheeks redder and fresher. On the third his white hair grew dark again. And by the time the fourth day had come he had the appearance of a handsome young man of five-and-twenty.

Now the princess, bewildered at first by the change in the two men, began to show signs of abhorrence for Aboul Fazil. On the first day she looked at him with disfavour, on the second she twitted him on his appearance, on the third she told him that he was like his own grandfather, and on the fourth she refused to look at him.

The nobles and pashas, observing her distaste for her former favourite, fell upon him and with cuffs and buffets expelled him from the court. And when the princess turned from Aboul Fazil in disgust, she began to take notice of Shadrach, who, day by day, was growing more handsome. And after a week had passed, on the very day when she was to have been united to the now loathsome Aboul, she was wedded to the hakim, to the joy of the Sultan and of the entire court who were assured of his wisdom and moderation.

"Sometimes the tortoise wins the race," said the first Imam.

"Especially if it can cast the shell from its back," laughed the second Imam.

*   *   *

After this deeply allegorical relation, it came as something of a shock to us all when a very Westernized Iraqi insisted that we all needed some light relief. "Did I ever tell you of the time I almost got married?" he asked.

Before anyone could stop him, he was telling us about the time he had finished some kind of geological activity in Arabia and had decided, as so many people of the East do, to spend some time in just travelling.

THE DESERT RAIDERS

I did not understand, (said the Iraqi) the true significance of the desert saying that "before the Most Accepted One of Allah there is much hardship," till I had reached the sand dunes up the way to the east of the Arabian Peninsula. Mine was not a mission of exploration. It was wandering, and a wanderer has no compass, so, accepting the philosophy of Stevenson, I pinned my faith to his dictum that to be moving is better than arriving.

Trekking up and down aimlessly as I was, I fell into the hands of bandits about whom much has been heard lately in Iraq. The only way to get out of their clutches was to play the brigand and then, watching the opportunity, make good one's escape. Three ruffians stood before me with loaded rifles. "I shall shed no blood if I become one of you," I said; and after that there was nothing for it but to fall into line.

I must explain that the Government of Iraq at that time had about as much authority in its south-western outposts as the London police have in the Scilly Isles. Caravans for Basra and Mecca were constantly passing across the tract to and from the Holy City. Those who pay tribute are immune. If they don't—well, sand doesn't leave many traces, even of holy green turbans. It has been said that the desert Arabs don't abuse fellow Moslems—about as much as Rob Roy didn't abuse fellow Christians, I fancy.

About a couple of days after I had unwillingly joined up, a rumour came to the camp that a caravan from Kuwait was crossing the desert to Medina, and that it would come by that part of the frontier where we were situated before striking south for the sacred places. Naturally the news aroused the wildest enthusiasm among the eighty-odd blackguards who composed our band. Life in the camp had been somnolent enough before, a matter of occasional scouting, interspersed with much coffee-drinking and smoking. Now scouts were going out in

124

every direction and an extraordinarily feverish activity prevailed. Even so, it was another three days before we got reliable news of the whereabouts of the caravan and this necessitated a camel ride of more than thirty miles.

It was at evening that we at last got our first sight of it, like a thin, black rope on the pale face of the desert, a moving thread of life among the sandhills. Down we swooped with a wild whooping calculated to scare the Zulus, and I cannot help laughing as I remember that in my nervousness of the ugly chieftain I gave vent to some of the most bloodcurdling yells ever heard outside of Greek drama.

The caravan came to a dead halt, and the ends drew back on the centre. Not a shot was fired, for the payment of tribute was the usual custom. Shortly we came up with our victims, who were obviously demoralized. The leader of the train rode out and explained to us that it was composed of exceptionally poor pilgrims who were unable to pay anything in the way of blackmail. In the name of the holy one, would the chief not allow them to pass?

But the chief had heard that story before. "We shall investigate their poverty," he said sternly, and then the fun began. Fat Hajis and portly merchants were man-handled and forced to part with their personal jewellery, money, and other belongings. Bales of costly merchandise were unwrapped and re-allocated. Camels of pedigree and valuable dromedaries were impounded. Fine Arab horses were examined for good points and were selected. And those who complained or resisted were beaten up and mauled. Cries of fear and indignation, curses and maledictions, resounded on all sides.

I saw the chief's eye on the man standing next to me. He strode up to a little wizened fellow who was making more uproar than half a dozen others. The Chief presented a rifle to his head.

"Pay up," he yelled, "or by the holy ones, I shall make you a leaden present."

"Brother," he moaned, "I have nothing, nothing, but the pure faith I take to the shrines, let the angels hear me."

"Off with your turban," said the chief menacingly, "or the devils will hear you quick."

Weeping and protesting, he drew off his greasy headgear.

Within was a handful of choice turquoises from Persia. On these the brigand chief swooped like a hawk, giving him a look almost of commendation.

It was a sorry train that we left in the desert as we rode away. But now came my opportunity. That night as the raiders sat in the moonlight dividing their loot, and much too busy at the job to think of anything else, I quietly mounted my camel and made off. By morning I was well on my way to Kuwait.

The day was hot and oppressive, but I was making record speed on my ship of the desert, till the fierce rays of the sun began to show some mercy and it was evening; one of those nights fell that you see only in the vast stretches of sand dunes: when all is quiet and the sky is jagged with dazzling points of light. And I slept the sleep of the bone weary.

I had been asleep only a short while when I awoke to find the business end of a long rifle rammed so hard into my neck as to be near breaking the skin. Struggling into a sitting posture, I saw a lean, dark face peering through the opening of my black tent covering.

"Hullo!" I said, "Take that shooting-iron away from my jugular, will you?"

"Peace be on you," said my visitor, "I thought for a moment you were an infidel."

"There is another think coming to you," I told him, "what's it all about?"

"Truly you are a man of strange words," replied my acquaintance, "do you not know in our country sleeping men are apt to be rudely awakened?"

I assured him that I had gathered the idea previously, but had resolved to ignore it. And as the trusting son of the desert laughed consumedly, I raised my foot and kicked him so hard on the knock-out part of the chin that he immediately dreamed of the planets. As nearly painless as might be, I roped him up, and knowing that some of his crowd would be along soon, took his camel and left him mine. His was a fleet one of the desert, one of the best, as I saw at a glance. The camel is, however, a froward beast. He will obey his master grudgingly, and being lawless at heart is only too prone to rebel against others. Before I had well mounted him, this demon of the desert made off like a tempest towards the place of sunrise, bumping me at every stride till I felt like the makings of an omelet.

Great Scott! But how that fleet brute careered over the burning desert. And then, just like a Margate donkey, he stopped dead, and I went over his long neck, ploughing my way down, down through a seeming ocean of hot sand.

When I came to the surface again, blaspheming in an argosy of several languages, and shaking the burning particles out of my eyes, ears and hair, I was amazed to hear a woman's voice greeting me. Now women unsponsored in the desert are about as rare as swallows in December, and I gazed through my watering eyes in amazement, until I saw by her dress and lack of veil that she was what is known as one of the Free Women of Arabia—a caste of ladies who for some reason or other have always been regarded with special reverence by the Bedouins, and who are not subject to their rather wearing social laws.

"And what can I do to help you?" I asked rather weakly.

"Your camel has gone," she replied smilingly, "and unless I give you a lift on mine you will have to remain here, so far as I can see."

"Very kind of you," I replied. "Come, let us be moving, for there are certain people in this vicinity who are looking for my heart's blood, and I haven't a drop to spare at the moment."

"I will take you on one condition," she said very firmly, "and it is that you take me to be your wife."

"But I thought a Free Woman never married!"

"That's just it " she remarked pettishly, "and I am tired of the single state."

Now I didn't want to splice up with the lady, and I knew it could be suicide to tell her I had a wife at home, so I merely nodded gravely. She made her camel kneel, I mounted behind, and off we went.

'Where do we go from here, Bulbul?" I asked.

"We go to Kuwait," she replied, "I want to see the Pictures, for the Inglis have brought the Magic Show; also my name is not Bulbul, but Khawala, so please remember."

The Pictures!. Five hours of clop-clopping through the sand to Kuwait on the Gulf; and then it must be the cinema at once, hungry and thirsty as I was. Night had fallen as we entered the movie house, and the interior was as dark as the cave of Eblis. So far, so good!

The film on the screen was one of those sob-stuff torments which turn some women into perfectly good understudies of Niobe for about six reels or so. My prophetic hopes, I found, were correct. Khawala was no exception to the rule. At the first sad caption she began to sniff, and when the Italian heroine writhed on a marble seat on reading the telegram that told of her lover's accident, she reached for my hand. Eventually, when the said lover returned on crutches, she broke down entirely, and laid her head on my shoulder.

"You are overcome," I whispered. "Let me get you some coffee, a cup will just put you right." A cup of coffee to an Arab woman is what a cup of tea is to her European sister, a never-failing solace.

Khawala peered up at me through the gloom. Her silver ornaments tinkled and dug me in the neck and cheeks.

"You are so good, dear," she murmured, "Yes, I think I should like a cup, but you won't be long, will you?"

Assuring her that I would not, I crept from the picture-house and made for the docks at greyhound speed. A felucca was in the act of weighing anchor for the port of Basra. The lateen sails were going up, and the anchor was half hauled in.

"Hi! Hi!" I called to the skipper. "Take me with you and I'll split a gold piece with you when we get to Basra."

"Jump then!" he cried "and save your neck if you can, for I can't put back."

I closed my eyes and jumped. A broken neck seemed a mild way out compared with what waited for me in the picture-house yonder.

For I should have told you that Khawala was forty-five if she was a day, that she had but three teeth in the upper jaw, and a smile like that on the face of a tiger. Her silver jewellery did not take a year off her age for all its fineness.

*　　*　　*

I said something about an apparent exploit having as much reality about it as a fairy-tale, when some of our companions asked me to tell them tales such as are known to the people of the West. When I had finished a concentrated version of *Cinderella*, a wizened ancient with a Mongolian cast of features spoke up.

"As a wandering dervish, I spent some years in a land which was occupied by the French Farangis, in the Farther East, called Indochine. They have a very old literature, and a tale which I can now tell you is to be found in books of theirs which were current over two and a half thousand years ago."

And this is what he told.

THE LEGEND OF TAM

Long, long ago there was a little girl named Tam. She lived with her father who was a widower. Then the father married again; and Tam's stepmother was a wicked woman. Tam discovered this on the very day following her father's second marriage. Naturally there was a big feast to celebrate, but little Tam was shut away in a small room all by herself. She could hear the music and the merry sounds of feasting, but she went hungry, and she was still hungry when she sought her couch.

Then the stepmother bore a daughter who was named Cam. She adored Cam as much as she hated Tam. The father was assiduously filled with lies about Tam; and the stepmother riled and riled against her, declaring that she wanted nothing whatever to do with such a despicable creature.

Tam had to live and work in a wretched place in the kitchen. She had nothing but a ragged quilt as a coverlet at night, and during her waking hours she was made to cook and to wash and to scrub floors and to do all the menial tasks which even the servants disdained to do. Her hands became red and blistered, but never once did she complain.

More than anything else did this sweet nature annoy the stepmother, who time after time sent Tam into the forests in the hope that she would be killed by wild beasts. She ordered the child to draw water from deep wells in the hope that she would fall in and be drowned. The poor girl just worked and worked. Her hair was in continual disarray, and she was not allowed the toilet requisites with which to wash. Beneath this disarray there was still little Tam, but all the world saw was a dirty, and ugly little girl.

But one day Tam found the opportunity to lave her face. Her stepmother saw, and was astonished. There was beauty beneath the disarray. More than ever was the stepmother aggravated, because she saw that Tam was indeed more beautiful than Cam.

130

One day the stepmother asked both Tam and Cam to go to the village pond to fish. To Tam, she said: "Get many fish. If you come back with only a few you will be whipped and sent supperless to bed."

By the end of the day Tam had a whole basketful of fish. Cam had none. She had spent the time picking flowers and sunning herself in the long grass. Even Cam did not like to go back without any fish so she said to Tam: "Sister, you hair is full of mud. Step into the clear water and wash it off; otherwise mother will be furious."

Tam stepped into the water and had a good wash. While she was so engaged Cam exchanged fish baskets, and hurried away home.

When Tam left the water and saw what had happened her cup was overflowing. She cried bitterly for she well knew of what her stepmother was capable.

Then she heard a sweet voice. "What is the matter, dear child?" it asked.

Then Tam saw. It was the Goddess of Mercy, blue-robed and smiling.

"Most Noble Lady," said Tam, "what am I to do? I have no fish—look, my sister Cam has taken them all."

But one tiny fish was left. It was still in the basket.

The Goddess of Mercy told Tam to take this tiny fish home and to put it in the well in the garden, and then to feed it three times a day with fragments from her own meals.

Tam did exactly as she was told, and every day when she went to the well the fish rose to greet her, but should anyone else ever appear the fish remained in the depths and never showed itself.

As always, the stepmother spied, and she noticed that a fish would appear for Tam and nobody else. She was both intrigued and annoyed, so she sent Tam on a distant errand.

Taking advantage of Tam's absence the stepmother put on some of Tam's ragged garments and went to the well. There she caught the fish, and took it to the kitchen where she cooked it and ate it.

When Tam returned from her errand she went to the well and called and called, but, of course, there was no fish. Tam was disconsolate. She wept and wept.

Again the Goddess of Mercy appeared to comfort her in her distress.

"I know what your stepmother has done," she told Tam. "She has killed and eaten your fish. But you must secure its bones and bury them under your sleeping mat. Then, whenever you are in need, pray to these bones, and your wish will be granted."

Tam nodded her head, and went to find the bones but they were missing.

"Cluck, cluck!" said a hen, "give me some rice, and I will show you the bones."

The hen got the rice, and waddled to the poultry yard. There she scratched at the earth and revealed the fishbones which had been buried by the stepmother.

When the autumn festival was due the stepmother filled a huge basket with red and green beans. "Sort these out" she demanded of Tam. "When you have completed the task you may go to the festival."

Then she and her daughter arrayed themselves in their best and went to the festival.

They had been gone for a long, long time and Tam, despairing of her task, lifted up a tearful voice and prayed: "O, Benevolent Goddess of Mercy, please help me," she sobbed.

At once the soft-eyed, blue-robed Goddess appeared. She bore in her hand the magic green willow branch. With this she turned small flies into sparrows, and in a twinkling the sparrows had performed Tam's task of sorting out the beans.

Tam dried her tears, and there before her eyes was a glimmering blue and silver dress fit for a Princess. At the smiling behest of the Goddess of Mercy she dressed herself in this and went to the festival.

Cam was the first to see this very beautiful lady.

"Who," she asked, "is that very rich lady so strangely like sister Tam?"

Tam saw that Cam and her stepmother were looking at her with strange expressions, and her old fears returned. She turned to run away, but in her hurry she dropped one of her fine slippers. This was retrieved by a soldier who took it to the King.

The King examined this piece of footwear very closely and declared that never before had he seen work so beautiful, so fine and so ravishing.

He held the slipper aloft, and bade the fair ladies present try to place it on their feet. But even those with the smallest feet were unable to do so.

Then he called together the wives of the nobles. They too were bade to try, but with similar ill-success.

Then he put round the word. Whomsoever could wear this slipper would become the Queen, the King's first wife.

Finally a timorous Tam was conducted to the presence, and of course the slipper fitted her perfectly. The King was captivated by her beautiful gown and the beauty of her features. She was taken to the palace with a sovereign's escort in attendance. In due course she became Queen and had a brilliant and happy life.

This the stepmother and sister could hardly bear. Willingly they would have killed Tam, but they were afraid of the King, and dared not.

One day, on the anniversary of her father's death, Tam went home to recite prayers for the departed on the altar of her father. On this day of the year custom demands that parents should receive obedience. The stepmother was well aware of this and she asked Tam to climb a tall areca tree to gather nuts for the guests. As she was good and pious, and well acquainted with tradition, she did not indignantly refuse to do this, because she was the Queen, but as the daughter, meekly acquiesced.

She sought to climb the tree, and while doing so was alarmed by the manner in which it lurched and swayed.

"What are you doing?" she called down to her stepmother.

"Child, I am only trying to scare away ants which would bite you," replied this scheming woman.

But in truth the stepmother was wielding an axe, and before long the tree fell, and the young Queen was killed immediately in the crash.

"Now, at long last we have got rid of her," exclaimed the stepmother with a hateful and ugly laugh. "We shall report to the King that his Queen died in an accident. I will offer my beloved Cam to the King that she may become Queen in her stead."

This scheme worked out as planned, and Cam indeed became the Queen; Tam's pure and innocent soul could find no sure rest. It had taken the shape of a nightingale which dwelt in a most beautiful grove in the King's garden. This nightingale sang especially sweet and melodious songs.

One day the King went to this particular grove and, as the handmaidens and ladies-of-honour exposed the ornately dragon-embroidered gown of the King to the rays of the sun, the nightingale sang in her special way.

"O, maids-of-honour," cried the Queen, "be careful with my husband's cloak. See that it does not come upon a thorn." But the entranced ladies of the Court heard her not. All their attention was diverted to the nightingale which now sang so softly that the King wept.

At last the King looked up from his tears.

"Most delightful nightingale," he exclaimed, "if it be that you are the soul of my late beloved Queen be pleased to settle in my wide sleeves."

The nightingale immediately did as the King asked, and rubbed her smooth head against the King's hand.

She was taken into the palace and lodged in a golden cage within the King's bedchamber. There, she sang more charmingly than before.

Naturally, Cam became very jealous of the nightingale, and she sought the advice of her mother.

One day, when the King was in Council, they entered the bed-chamber, seized the nightingale and took it to the kitchens. There they killed it and ate it, and threw the feathers into the King's garden.

The King was enraged when he saw the empty cage and demanded explanations.

"Perhaps she had become bored. Perhaps she has flown away to the woods," ventured the guilty Cam. The King remained very sad at his loss, but there was nothing he could do. But once again Tam's restless soul manifested itself. This time her soul had taken on the form of a beautiful tree which bore but a single fruit. It was round and golden, and gave off a very sweet smell.

An aged women spied this fruit, picked it up and took it home in her bag.

Next day, to her complete astonishment, she found her house spruce and tidy. Next day she hid herself, and she beheld a slim and beautiful lady emerging from the fruit. As the lady engaged in her task of tidying the abode, the old woman rushed to the fruit and tore it asunder, so that the slim and beautiful occupant could not return. Thus the young creature had to stay in the house, where she regarded the old woman as her mother.

One day, the King was on a hunting expedition, and lost his way. As evening was nigh he sought shelter, and this was at the old woman's house.

According to custom, the King was offered betel. He noticed the delicate manner in which this had been prepared, and said:

"Who has done this? This is prepared just in the same way as my Tam used to prepare it."

In a trembling voice the old woman replied: "Sire, it has been prepared only by my unworthy daughter."

The King ordered the daughter into his presence and when she came and bowed, the King realised, as in a dream, that once more he was in the presence of his beloved Tam.

Tam was taken back to the palace where she was restored to her position as Queen, and this time it was Cam who was entirely neglected.

Cam pondered. She knew that she was not as beautiful as Tam, but she approached her sister.

"Dearest Queen, how can I become as white as you?" she asked.

"It is very easy," Tam replied. "You have only to jump into a big basin of boiling water, to become beautifully white."

Cam believed this, with inevitable results.

When the stepmother heard of the distressing episode she wept and wept until she became blind. Soon she, too, died of a broken heart. Tam survived them both, and lived happily ever after.

*   *   *

Which all goes to show that we may search in vain for national copyrights in traditional lore. Indeed, it is possible that the folktale is almost the sole common property of mankind, accessible and acceptable to all, regardless of the things which divide us one from another.

Nearing Medina the Illuminated, the City of the Prophet, a

sense of excitement mounted among the jaded caravaneers. But this was tempered by the rumour, brought us by local beduins, that there were bandits about. To take our minds off this—or perhaps to keep us alert—a Persian companion asked permission, with that courtesy which many Persians have, to relate the story of Suleiman, the Brigand.

WOMAN AS THE SHADOW OF MAN

By no stretch even of the most romantic imagination could the cavern of Suleiman, the brigand, be described as one befitting his reputation. It was small, dark, and decidedly damp, yet in this sordid den the predatory chieftain, with whose name northern Persia rang, took such ease as he permitted himself.

It was a dismal afternoon in the rainy season. The wind wailed outside through the screen of stunted pines which face the cave, and blew the smoke of the tiny fire which burned at its entrance over the head and shoulders of the bandit, so that it seemed as a veil round the torso of a mysterious adept.

What Suleiman was actually doing it would be hard to say. Ask what a statue is engaged in, and you probably have the reply. He might have been sleeping, he might have been thinking. But when the noise of footsteps on the twig-lined path outside crackled in his hearing, he became sufficiently alive, and raised a bearded and hawk-nosed face out of the folds of a huge camel-hair cloak.

A woman stood by the fire, veiled, and as motionless as himself. Such visits were more than infrequent in Suleiman's experience. He had not set eyes on a female form for quite a quarter of a year, yet he remained immovable. It was his invariable custom to permit visitors the first move.

"You are Suleiman?" the lady asked, keeping her face veiled.

The brigand bowed. "You have come to ransom some-one?" he asked carelessly. "The tea-merchant perhaps?"

The shrouded form swayed a little. "No, I come on quite another errand," was the reply. "I have heard that Suleiman occasionally assists those in distress. Is it not so?"

"Such has happened," admitted the brigand.

"Ah, but this time there is no possibility of refusal," cried the veiled lady urgently. "Suleiman has been branded as a coward. Will he accept the dishonour?"

Suleiman leapt to his feet, an oath on his bearded lips. Every man has his limit of endurance, and he had never in his life been taunted with poltroonery. The experience was a strange one and his blood burned to liquid flame. In a couple of strides he crossed to where his visitor stood, and with a single action he tore the veil from her head. It revealed a vision of terrified beauty at which he stepped back amazed—great luminous eyes gleaming in a face of golden fairness, quivering lips of loveliness, a forest of wavy hair. But frightened as she was, the lady still evidently retained courage enough to go through with her mission.

"That has touched you, Suleiman the Black," she laughed, "you may think me a fool to brave you in your fastness, but my husband is a prisoner—and what will a true woman not do for her husband?"

"You speak in riddles," growled Suleiman. "Come to the point."

"My husband, the Sirdar Jafar, is, or was, a general in the army of the Shah; you have heard of him. The rebels have taken him prisoner. They have not only loaded him with chains, and treated him foully, but have accused him of cowardice, saying that his defeat was due to panic. He was inconsolable at the charge, and in his wrath has flung to them a challenge. He has undertaken, if they set him free, to capture you single-handed—that is, unless you prefer to come down under safe-conduct to Tehran and face him sword in hand, as man to man."

Suleiman stared. Then he laughed, loud and long.

"The impertinence of your proposal is amazing," he cried at last. "Am I to be the fool of any soldier who desires to vindicate his honour?"

"You recognize the alternative?" said the woman scathingly. "You will be branded as a coward through the length and breadth of Persia. How will Suleiman the Black relish such a name?"

"After all, I am a bandit, one who lives on plunder. Should I prevail, what is my reward?"

"The reward," answered the woman dully, "is myself, for so I have agreed with my lord. Will not that suffice?"

Suleiman the Black started. "Truly," he said, not without

admiration, "you must love your lord. But, foolish one, what is there to prevent me from keeping you here if I wish, which, by the way, I have no particular desire to do?"

"Your manhood," was the curt reply, "which I am confident even a Suleiman has not altogether lost. Your answer?"

Suleiman laughed once more, shortly this time. "You have won," he said. "I shall go with you to the capital and shall fight the Sirdar Jafar."

Tehran at the commencement of the year 1700 was by no means the Tehran of today. Its old time atmosphere pervaded it. The schools and colleges were closed, the airport was not there, the various ministries teemed not with up-to-date officials in European dress. Instead, the spirit of the backward East was triumphant. Long-robed mullahs and bearded tribesmen in turban and sheepskin prowled the streets.

Said, the general of the then Shah, might confidently be described as of the older school. As he sat sipping coffee with his *Kalyan* at full blast, he would have provided an excellent study for an artist in search of a human example of the unchanging East. Squatting on a cushion, he seemed to be dead rather than to live. It was only in the midst of battle that he ever really woke up. Even at the subsequent division of loot he appeared somnolent, though no one ever dreamed of cheating him. That would have been about as sensible as to snatch a lamb from between the jaws of a tiger. But now he was to receive news which would awaken him.

"Sirdar—my father," said one approaching him with a low salaam, "The lady Kulsum, wife of Jafar, has returned, bringing with her Suleiman the Black."

The mouthpiece of his *Kalyan* fell from Said's bearded lips. "By the hoof of the Father of Evil!" he cried, "but a strange thing has come to pass. That the wolf of the hills should descend to the city!" And Said marvelled all the more, because he too had been a brigand. "Bring them before us," he commanded.

They came, lady and bandit, the one closely veiled, as the old order provided, the other grave, not unsmiling. They stood before Said in silence.

"Suleiman," rasped the General, "what is this? Know you what you do?"

"She who is with me has told me all," replied the bandit. "I

139

fight with Jafar. Should I conquer, she falls to my lot; should I fail . . ."

"Then a brigand has his pride?" laughed Said very sourly.

"My lord should know," answered Suleiman making obeisance. "When do I fight Jafar?"

"At once if you so choose," grunted the General, "and you have the right to make conditions. You have been branded as a coward, a serious charge. Will you fight on foot or on horseback, with the sword or with the long rifle?"

"With the sword and on horseback," said the brigand roughly. "Bring forth your defeated enemy, and let us see what sort of a man has dared to dub Suleiman the Black as a poltroon."

If the city had seemed somnolent when Suleiman and the lady Kulsum entered it, it grew lively enough when the news that a combat was impending gained currency. Thousands gathered on the broad green space without the gates, and it was all that a strong guard of Said's irregulars could do to prevent the mob from swarming over the field.

At last the combatants appeared. Suleiman on a fast white Arab, silent, confident in poise; Jafar on a bright bay, in the uniform of the Shah's army, broad-chested, yet elegant. Both reined their steeds before the seat of Said the General.

"This," boomed Said sententiously, "is a combat of honour. The ex-General Jafar, accused of cowardice, has offered to free himself from the charge by fighting the brigand Suleiman, whom men call 'the Invincible,' and whose courage none has ever questioned. The combat is, therefore, bound to be one to the death. Let it begin forthwith."

At the word the combatants wheeled their horses, rode some fifty yards from the General's seat, and, setting spurs, dashed at each other. Clashing, their scimitars met in the air like silver streaks, then played lightly above their heads in fantastic radiance in the afternoon sunlight. Suleiman sat his saddle easily, like a cavalier; the Sirdar Jafar, more heavily, as a trained horseman, yet doggedly, rising now and then for the vantage of a stroke. Round and round each other they circled, neither having the advantage, each fencing for an opening. Then the Sirdar's blade fell like the beak of a hawk, and a thin stream of blood trickled down the bandit's left arm. The crowd roared.

"A shrewd stroke," muttered Said like a connoisseur, "had it been the sword arm. . ."

The brigand chief gave back, drawing careful rein, evidently heeding not at all his hurt. Then, suddenly, he charged, smote, and Sirdar Jafar rolled from the saddle, an ugly gash on his brow. He staggered, wiped his forehead with a gilded sleeve, and, on foot as he was, rushed at his adversary, his teeth clenched, his eyes gleaming through the blood pouring down his face.

But Suleiman spurred and avoided him, then springing from his horse, advanced to meet him. That both men were sorely hurt was obvious to the onlookers. Said glanced at the Lady Kulsum, who, still closely veiled, stood silent and statuesque.

"Now," said Suleiman to himself, as he warded off the blows of the bleeding Sirdar. "What does the woman wish? Truly there is no comprehending women. If I kill her husband, she will detest me. If I allow him to kill me, she will remember me as a weakling. Which is the worse! The curse of Sheitan on it, but I cannot get those eyes of hers out of my head. Bah, I must resort to an ancient trick."

The weapons met, clashed, and Jafar's fell, his right hand with it, severed at the wrist by a single sweeping back-blow. Suleiman's sleight of swordsmanship had served him well.

That evening, with safe conduct, the brigand and the Lady Kulsum rode out of Tehran. When at last the guards left them Suleiman turned to her.

"You seem displeased, lady," he said with a grave smile. "Yet I did what a man might in the circumstances. I saved the life of your lord, mine own honour and his. What would you? Now I offer you your freedom. Go back to him and you will."

"I do not break my word," she replied sombrely. "A woman has her honour too. I am willing to pay the price."

"I am a bandit," replied Suleiman, "not a torturer. You are free to return to your husand."

"To an armless man!" she retorted.

"All the more reason why you should return to him," said the brigand roughly. "You will provide him with hands."

They rode on in silence for some time. It was sunset, the shadows of night were gathering.

"Perhaps," said the Lady Kulsum. "Perhaps I do not wish to return to Tehran."

"Woman," murmured Suleiman, as if to himself, "is, after all, but the shadow of man. Where he is there must she be also, and the greater the man, the greater she, the shadow."

At this the Lady Kulsum seemed strangely agitated. "Truly," she said haughtily, "that man has need of all his manliness who wears his bugle by his side and blows it often to arouse his own courage, to awake his belief in himself. That, at least, Jafar never did."

"Bah!" chuckled Suleiman with a sour smile, "now that he hath no hand to raise his bugle. . ."

"Coward," she flashed, "To belittle a better man, whom, after all, you conquered by a brigand's trick of fence."

"Silence," hissed Suleiman. "You are now my slave, and impertinence in a brigand's slave is usually punished by the lash."

Kulsum grew pale. "What mean you?" she asked incredulously. "The lash?"

"Aye, the lash, which your handless husband could not give you." Suleiman was very harsh now. "A daily dose of that. . ."

"Oh," cried she, reining in, "this is intolerable. I believed you to be a cavalier at least, if an untamed one. But I find you only a brute. I shall return to Tehran."

"Not so," and Suleiman caught at her bridle. "You have made your bed and must lie thereon. Another word, woman, and I lay my whip across your back."

On and on they rode, now through the darkness of the night. The blackness of a deep crevasse loomed before them. Suleiman loosed the rein he held.

"I shall ride on in front a little," he announced. "This place is dangerous, for the chief who guards it has no compunction in killing travellers, be they merchant or bandit. Follow me."

He pressed forward into the darkness, and when he had ridden some fifty yards, halted and waited. He did not hear the Lady Kulsum following. Indeed, he heard the noise of a horse galloping quickly away in the opposite direction.

Suleiman rose in his stirrups and laughed a great laugh. "It is well," he said, "for I did not want her. They are all the same. Throw them one kind word, and they will follow you to Sheol, but growl at them. . ."

And, well content, he cantered back to his cavern. The fire was lit, and, weary, he cast himself on the couch of dry grass.

He was on the verge of sleep, when he heard someone clamber up the slope. Rising, he sought the entrance and looked out into the night. Kulsum stood before him. He started forward.

"You!" he said.

"Yes, lord. Woman is but the shadow of man."

The brigand cursed heartily. "I wished you away," he foamed, "so I dissembled. Know that I could not chasten you if I would. I am not the savage you think me. Begone, return to Tehran, for, verily, I have played a part, have lied to you, because I would be alone."

"It is not good that you should be alone," she said decidedly, "for a shadowless man is a man bewitched, so I shall stay here. In Tehran there is nothing for me, for I hate the cities. And the spirit of woman craves for the wild. I shall cook your food and care for your wants, my lord," and she made obeisance to him.

"Now," said Suleiman to himself, "this is my punishment, but, by my guardian angel, it is much too severe." And aloud he said: "As thou wilt, woman, but I pray you, be gentle with my belongings here, nor disturb this place any more than the devil which possesses all woman tempts thee to do."

And the Lady Kulsum, glancing round at the confusion of the cavern, smiled the age-long smile of woman, which is the doom of such comfortable confusion.

*   *   *

In Medina we were joined by an Afghan diplomat and military man who wanted our company on the way to Mecca, and I wondered whether he would have a tale to contribute to our now rich saga. But he shook his head and insisted that he did not know any stories, as these were, he felt, really for children: although I reminded him that for most of human history children were about the only people who did not listen to tales, which were passed down by specialists to the adults of every community for a variety of purposes.

Then, suddenly, as we were resting in a half-ruined house

north of Mecca, he said: "This place, with its desolate air, does put me in mind of something which happened to me when I was working on some documents with a Scandanavian called Rask, many years ago."

I called together some of the other pilgrims, and this is what we then heard.

THE MAGIC HOUSE

My friend Rask and I rented an ancient house in the Afghan uplands to do some literary research. Legend had it that it was built by one of the Princes of Kafiristan for an Indian woman who had strange beliefs. The inner walls of one of the rooms were covered with hard cement and painted over in the similitude of flames: red and yellow-topped. We used it as a study.

Rask, an expert in Sanskrit, read an old inscription over the door, started to behave in a strange manner, and asked me to go away for one night. I went to Kabul.

His insistence that I should not return on that night had the precise effect of making me resolved to do so. Try as I might I could not shake off an odd feeling of restlessness as I returned to the cottage, the *Jamma,* or Place of Collection.

So dark an October night had it grown that for a moment or two I failed to discern the house, although it could not have been more than a mile away, but at length I espied its shape and at once I noticed that the window of our room was brightly lit.

As I drew near I was at first astonished, then alarmed, to notice that what I had taken for a brilliant illumination now seemed like the glow of a furnace. I broke into a run, and at every step the blaze seemed to grow more intense. Four hundred metres away from the cottage I could see through the unshuttered windows the furious glare of a great conflagration. The interior of the room resembled a seething cauldron of flame, and a roaring sound borne on the still night air completed the assurance that what I beheld was a fire of no ordinary kind but a veritable maelstrom of flaming destruction.

There was no answer to my call, but from behind the door of the painted room came the tumult of a great burning. I beat upon it with both hands, calling upon my friend. That he was inside some instinct assured me. In an agony of terror I tore at

145

the handle and wrenched the door open.

As I did so the surging roar ceased with startling suddenness. I dashed into the room. There lay Rask, or what at first seemed a charred heap in his likeness. I carried him to his bedroom and tore his smouldering clothes from his scorched body.

During the next few days I nursed him, and during that time had a full opportunity of examining the painted room. It bore not the slightest trace of burning, but I noticed that the walls had been drenched with whitewash or something similar and that the painted flames which had covered them were now only partly visible.

Weeks passed before Rask was well enough to tell me what had happened; and then I listened to one of the strangest stories it has been my lot to hear.

The inscription said: "Nalla the pious, the servant of Durga, makes this gift of painted walls to the goddess, so that it may blaze annually on the day of her festival, and may consume any who dares to defile the sanctity of her shrine."

Durga is a form of Kali, Hindu goddess of destruction. "The expatriate Hindu lady, desirous of propitiating the goddess in the manner peculiar to her caste, that is, by lighting a great fire in her honour once a year, and consuming within it human beings or animals, and unable to accomplish her pagan intentions in this country, adopted magical means of doing so," said Rask.

"Magical means?" I said, "I don't follow you."

"I am not surprised. But you must bear with me. As you know, in many countries and especially in ancient Egypt and India, that which is painted is believed to possess a latent quality of reality, which only requires the urgency of a spell, or incantation, to render it actively existent. Nalla piously prays that the painted walls may flash in flames at a stated period every year; that is, on the anniversary of the goddess she adored. I found that it takes place at this time. I remembered that one of the ancient ways of cleansing a heathen shrine is by the application of quicklime to its walls. I used garden lime.

"The fire, which was increasing as I worked, finally overcame me. It must have been a quarter of an hour before you came that I found the temperature of the room growing intolerable. I remember staggering to the door, but as I reached it a spurt of flame flashed from the wall opposite me and barred my passage. A volume of noxious gas seemed to envelop me, and I lost consciousness. Why I should have been burnt and the fabric of the room left undamaged is, I think, explained by the magical nature of the fire . . ."

"But all this does not explain why the fire ceased so suddenly when I entered the room," I said.

"That does not perplex me much," replied Rask.

"All students of the occult know that a manifestation which may persist in the presence of one person often ceases if another enters the scope of its activity. Probably the reason that the phenomenon did not become visible before it did was that we were almost constantly together in the room."

* * *

This was the last tale given us before we entered the Holy City, where the rituals of the pilgrimage occupied our complete attention thenceforth. I have dealt with these experiences in my book *Westward to Mecca*, and I will not therefore repeat them here.

But Mecca is full of Afghans; they often retire here for reasons of piety, after a lifetime spent in the harsher climes of Central Asia. So it was not surprising that, after completing my religious obligations and making a trip to Riyadh to see the King, I found an old friend from home in the city, who invited me to his house. When I spoke of our relating stories during the long march from Turkey, he asked whether I knew the tale of Ahmed and Zara and Sadiq the Rich. As I did not, he lost no time in beginning.

NIGHT RIDE FROM KANDAHAR

"As clouds conceal the moon," said Ahmed, to his friend Suleiman, "so do those curtains hide the loveliest face in Kandahar."

Suleiman shook his head. "Why torment yourself," he asked, "knowing as you do that your Zuleikha is to be given to old Sadiq in three day's time? His wealth holds you in its grip as a strong wrestler might clutch a weakly child. You can do nothing, Ahmed, but curse fortune."

"That has not been the way of my Afghan forebears," sneered Ahmed, his strong white teeth showing in a snarl like a cheetah's. "As you say, I have three days, and within the compass of that round I shall free my Zuleikha from the terror of this gilded ancient, or—or, Suleiman, there will be one less of my race in Kandahar."

Suleiman frowned, for he was a lawyer, and therefore did not like threats.

"No violence, Ahmed, my brother," he begged. "You know that the vengeance of the new Amir is swift as death by the white poison of the Feringhees."

"Life without the moon of my desire would be too long were it but a day," cried Ahmed, with passion in his eyes. "So I care not what betides if she is not to be mine."

The moon, to which rather fulsome poetical allusion had been made in the Afghan manner, pushed clear of the thin clouds at this very moment, and flooded the garden as white wine falls into a glass.

"Is she not like a lily unfolding her petals in the pool of night?"

"Who?" laughed Suleiman, "the moon or your lady-love? Your allegories follow so closely in the steps of Hafiz, my Ahmed, that my simple mind I—"

"*Your* simple mind, my good fee-snatcher," jibed his friend. "Off to your bed and dream of writs and costs, while I—"

148

"While you play the prince from the Arabian Nights under this casement. As you will, foolish son of a wise father."

"Who himself was once a foolish son," whispered Ahmed, as he turned to the balcony, and began to climb to it by the thick creepers which hugged the wall.

The noise of his ascent had evidently been heard, and the casement was cautiously opened. He entered through the small aperture thus made, noiselessly and like a shadow.

"Your lips, star of my days, your lips!"

For answer, a small hand covered his mouth.

"If you would not become the food of scimitars," whispered a rich low voice, "you will remain dumb as Adoub, whose tongue was eaten by the dogs of Samarkand."

"You—you are not Zuleikha?" stammered Ahmed.

"Nor did I say I was," came the shattering answer, "I am her friend Zara, arrived here these two hours only. She, poor gazelle, is— is gone."

"Gone!" Ahmed almost gulped the word in his agony. "Gone, what mean you by that?"

"Why gallant sir, 'gone' expresses itself. The word has but one meaning. If you ask where she has gone I can tell you, for she charged me do so. Not an hour since she was carried to the house of Sadiq the merchant. She is there even now."

"Then you, by the might of the Compassionate, you are, of course, Sadiq's daughter. She has spoken to me of you."

"None other, my young hero," said the girl mockingly, "who likes this marriage as little as yourself. My father rejoiced to leave me here with Zuleikha's women, knowing my distaste for the match."

His passionate grief slowly hardened to a terrific purpose, shining and brightening as does the diamond in the agony of the earthquake from mere carbon into final adamant. "Then it is plain, delectable Zara, what we must do," he urged thickly, "I must bear you off and hold you prisoner until your father agrees to let Zuleikha go. He cannot wed her for three days, according to the law, even though she be in his house, the old fox."

Zara sighed, then laughed. "The plan is a good one, even though you are not over-polite about my father," she said, "I will raise no objection, although, my handsome soldier, it will

149

scarcely add to my reputation to be borne away by such a cavalier as your illustrious self."

"What may you do in the face of force?" asked Ahmed stubbornly.

"Or in that of manly beauty?" retorted Zara with a giggle.

"Pah," cried Ahmed, "spare me your jibes, lady. The business is a desperate one. My horse is tethered not so far away and soon we can be at my pavilion in the hills. Come." And, raising her in his arms, he scrambled lightly to the ground.

Through night-bound Kandahar they galloped on his white mare, ghosts speeding towards the grey hills. The hooves ate up the miles of this moonlit region, a fairy canter though a silvery paradise.

The hills drew nearer, vast shapes throwing out long arms in which to hide the escapaders. It was the hills that seemed to gallop, not the tiny horse with its double burden, which, in relation to their hugeness, appeared almost to stand still to meet them.

At last, after two hours' riding, they came to Ahmed's pavilion in the glen. Not a light was there. All was silent as water unruffled by wind. He unlocked the door, and they entered. He struck a match and lit a single lamp.

"This," said Zara, "is what one might expect from a soldier who is also a poet." She was petite and dark, the antithesis to the fair and ruddy beauty of his Zuleikha. He looked at her with some disfavour. Lord, but he was the very son of folly after all, to have carried off this daughter of a rich and powerful father to the hills. And what would his Zuleikha think about it?

"I—I have been mad," he stuttered. "I had no right to bring you here. We must return to Kandahar."

She threw herself wearily on a divan. "Is it not strange that a woman's fatigue is stronger than a man's might? You may return if your please—if you are so discourteous—"

Her voice trailed away in a sleepy murmur. She was paler than ivory in the night, than the heart of the moon herself, yet dusky of hair and lashes as the forest which lofted above the roof under which they rested. For the first time in all his days he was alone with a strange woman—utterly alone.

After all, the fault was his. Yet, was it? Had he not fallen into a trap, brother of madness that he was? What a pass was his! He was held fast on both horns of perplexity. This girl would be searched for, the countryside would be scoured for her. He could not but be suspect. The punishment for carrying off a marriageable girl was one of the most rigorous in the Fundamental Law of Afghanistan. Surely he was doomed.

His fear was hunted from him by a sudden savage suspicion. Yes, this girl had surely been an instrument: to lure him to leave Kandahar where his beloved, the soul of his soul, was in danger. Well, he would discover the plot. Snatching a Persian dagger from the wall, he stooped and seized Zara by the rippling treasure of her long dark hair.

She opened her sleepy eyes and stared at him in terror. The short night of the Afghan summer came to an end with almost miraculous swiftness and the room was suddenly drenched by the rising sun with the colour of blood.

"What would you do?" cried Zara faintly, her eyes fixed upon the dagger as one looks upon a serpent about to strike.

"Punish a traitor," he cried vehemently. "You have betrayed me and Zuleikha, your own friend. You know well that she never charged you with the false message you gave to me."

He made to strike. Looking at his eyes, she could well believe that he intended to make her blood mingle on the Persian rugs with the scarlet hues of sunrise.

"In the name of the Merciful," she cried, "as one day you would see the face of the Holy One, hearken to me, spare me, and I will confess all to you."

He lowered his arm. He loosed his grip upon her hair. She rose from her knees and stood before him, close, so close that he could feel her breath upon his lips, like a breeze blown from the rose-gardens of Saadi's Gulistan.

"Speak," he said, "but if you speak a lie, you shall not live to see the sun in his full glory. Already his hair brushes the threshold of the world. Not long shall it be, then, till the whole majesty of his face appears."

"I—I must speak what is shameful, then," she murmured, "but it shall be the truth, I swear by Azrael, the angel of death. I—I love you, Ahmed—have loved you for months in secret. I it was who urged my father Sadiq the Rich to take Zuleikha from her father's house tonight. Then I betook myself to her house unknown to anyone, in the hope that you—oh, that you might do as you have done, bear me off as a hostage. You have the truth. Now strike, if you will, for it is more bitter than myrrh for a woman to confess love to him who hates her."

Ahmed stood confounded, his great brown eyes gazing at her in vast bewilderment.

"And Zuleikha?" he gasped.

"Was wed to my father Sadiq ere she left her father's house. The rites have been ratified for days."

He cried out, as though the dagger he held had been thrust into his bosom. Casting it from him, he covered his face with his hands, and staggered to the divan, where he lay in a crumple of abandoned grief.

"I have been doubly betrayed," he cried, "by you and by the woman whom I love."

"Not so," she answered. "Zuleikha has surely betrayed you, for from the first she had an eye to my father's wealth, to the great rubies of my dead mother, to a luxury of living such as you, a soldier, could not give her. But I have betrayed you not, since in love all is fair."

"There shall be vengeance for this," he panted.

"You talk like a man in an old song," she laughed, "leave such maunderings to the heroes of ballads and epics. People don't get broken hearts nowadays, you know."

"Because they have no hearts to break." His voice was bitter as the early mountain wind which blew in at the open casement.

To his amazement he saw that she was weeping. The molten crystal of the tears rained down her cheeks.

"No heart to break!" she cried, "and you can say this for whom I have ventured all? Never dare I return to my father's house after tonight."

"The fool must bear the burden of his folly," he quoted harshly. "Can you expect that I shall wed with a woman who has so wronged me—with the daughter of the man who stole from me the heart of my very heart?"

'And is not part of the blame and the folly yours, O my soldier?" She looked wearily at him through her tears.

"I admit the haste of my decision," he agreed, "but remember that you lied to me. Indeed, how may I know that you have not doubly lied? What proof have I, after all, that

Zuleikha is wedded to your father?"

"I swear it by the name which may not be spoken," she whispered, raising her hand dramatically. "But greatly now do I fear for myself—for both of us. Since you detest me so deeply, Ahmed, take me back to Kandahar before my absence is discovered and vengeance follows."

He realized the awful peril of both. As a man he must act and that at once. But he could not carry this woman back to the city on horseback in daylight.

"I will disguise you as my groom," he told her. "You will darken your face and follow me on the hill-pony which I will bring from the paddock out yonder."

"Alas," she moaned, "I cannot manage a horse."

"Then I can do but one thing—carry you farther into the mountains, and hand you over to a friendly enemy of mine, the chief of one of the hill tribes. He will probably make you one of his inferior wives, a kind of privileged servant, and you will have to milk goats and make cheeses for the rest of your days—a fate much too good for such as you."

The great dark eyes opened wide in horrified amazement, then narrowed in contempt.

"You would sell me," she gasped, "to a barbarian?"

"Nay not sell you, for who would buy a woman who has already betrayed a man? But haste, we have far to go, and we must first eat."

He brought little cakes, butter and the sour Koumiss, and in silence they ate and drank. Then, when he had taken a rifle and bandolier from the wall, he beckoned her to follow him. His white mare stood tethered to the post, cropping the grass in a circle, and after he had watered the beast, he swung Zara to its withers, and mounted.

On they sped down the donga through the bright, chill early morning, wordless, each wrapt in angry thought. He cared not what chanced to her, she understood that all she had risked had been cast away. She knew romance to be a lie. What, indeed, was life but a lie?

The fatalism of her people gripped her like the embrace of a giant. Yet, even in that titanic grasp, she stirred and struggled as women have ever done, loathing the idea of the monstrous thing which was about to happen to her. There was just one

153

way out of the wretchedness of such a lot—death. But, even as she thought of it, she shuddered. Death is a fable to the ears of youth, which when it comes to be considered, takes on the colours of a tale too horrible for thought.

Ahmed's mind wandered in the mists of the desert of confusion. He neither knew nor cared whence he was going. Motion, action, were essential to his present condition of mind. Movement was a drug, an anodyne, to dull the ache at his heart. Once he stooped and peered deeply into the dark and wonderful face so near to his. He shivered, but not only from the chill morning air.

Thus they went forward for perhaps an hour, through remote valleys like the corridors of sleep, whose mists were mingled with the sun's first gold. Then, to his practised ear, came the thud-thud of hoofs on the yielding turf. Was it pursuit? It could not be, for the noise of it came from beyond, and not behind them.

That sound he recognized only too well. It was the drumming made by the ponies of raiding hillmen. He checked his horse and waited. Round the elbow of the rise came three mounted men, galloping like the wind, moss-troopers of the valleys, seeking other men's horses, other men's cattle to drive back to their hill-forts.

As they caught sight of his uniform they reined up into sudden immobility like cavaliers in bronze against a background of heath and grey-golden air. They then dismounted, and pulling their horses into a recumbent position, crouched behind them, their long *jezail* rifles at the present. In Ahmed they beheld their natural enemy, a soldier, and although they feared not a dozen such, they were wise in their craft and were taking no chances.

Ahmed had just time to leap from the saddle, drag Zara after him, and pull his horse to the turf when a puff of smoke, beautiful as a white rose, jetted from the rifle of the nearest bandit. A bullet sang to the left, and the soldier, returning the fire, saw a dark form leap up from behind the huddled horseflesh which protected it, and fall back to the ground in an ungainly heap.

A second shot rang out like the crack of a whip, multiplying itself into a hundred echoes as it rattled down the vale. The ball struck the earth harmlessly between the pair who crouched low behind the white horse.

They looked at one another, and, for the first time since their meeting, they smiled. He saw that her lips were firm, her eyes clearly unafraid.

"Lie low," he commanded roughly. "Take cover."

"Why should I care, having lost all?" she asked bitterly. "A bullet now would be the best friend I could find."

He took cool and careful aim at the second hillman, or at what he could see of him, when the strengthening sun glanced on the curve of a shaven skull. He pulled lightly on the trigger.

Rat-at-at. The head bobbed up and disappeared. Ahmed laughed. The sights of Government rifles were more efficient than the antique points of the *jezail*, after all!

A cry from Zara arrested him as he made to fire at the third man. All he saw was a little thick white smoke, concealing man and horse for a moment. Then a small lithe body hurtled in front of his own. For a few seconds it lay there rigidly, while he strove to disentangle himself, and then it suddenly relaxed.

The hillman rose with a laugh, thinking that his ball had found the intended mark. An instant later he was rolling down the slope with a bullet in his brain. Ahmed turned anxiously to Zara, who seemed lifeless. In the round whiteness of her left shoulder blazed the jagged wound made by a *jezail* bullet, from which the blood welled slowly.

Frenziedly he made a wad of his handkerchief, tore off his sash, and bound up the wound. As he did so her eyes opened slowly and gazed into his.

"You still think me treacherous?" she asked. As she spoke she raised her head slightly. He bent downward and kissed her, long and passionately.

The wound, he saw, was not a dangerous one, being close to the shoulder-bone, but it must be staunched without loss of time. Raising her tenderly, he placed her once more on the white horse's withers and mounting, rode back to his pavilion at a careful canter.

That night, after help had been procured, and Zara was already on a fair way to recovery, Ahmed interviewed Sadiq the Rich. The words between the men were few but satisfactory.

"Young man," said the merchant, "you have won a heart

that loves you and lost a heart that loves only itself. Are you not thus fortunate? And when I die, much of my wealth shall go to Zara my daughter. So be doubly comforted."

But it was not in such considerations alone that Ahmed found his comfort.

* * *

The East is full of tales which underline how strange is the way of life which sometimes makes good come out of intended evil—though yet forbidding the conscious exercise of that which is itself wrong. That this operates on the psychological plane, within the mind of man, just as surely as in social affairs in the round, has long been known and accepted in our lands.

As I was pondering this, a man of Pakistan among us, a dervish, spoke.

"The human brain is full of ideas and potential actions which the ancients discovered how to render in terms perceptible by us through tales. A human tendency in a man, or woman, may reveal itself in speech or action, just as surely as the Qadi in the story revealed himself to those out to kill him. In such a way, the mental feature may, fortunately or otherwise, cause its own 'death.'"

And, on our asking, Bashir Mohammed the Dervish gave us the story of The Qadi's Cloaks.

THE QADI'S CLOAKS

Sitting cross-legged on the floor, Qadi Jalal applied a little more henna to his usually snow-white beard. Then he looked in the mirror.

"My flaming red beard should please my third wife," he thought with great personal satisfaction. From time to time he leaned back to obtain a clearer view of his handiwork, then forward, to put the close gaze of direct scrutiny upon the venture.

None could see the occupation of the Qadi, because he was in a locked room at the time, but few would have believed the evidence of their eyes if they had; for the benign smile which creased his face as he finished the final undermost strand would have been the very first that they had ever witnessed him indulge in.

Jalal's mind, however, was not completely occupied with the business in hand. It was partly on a small bag lying beside him on the floor.

"I'll let the hands of that young scoundrel be cut off, as was my sentence, so that the next time he wants to pick pockets he will have but feet with which to do it." Jalal wasn't the Sultan's judge for nothing.

And his eyes narrowed as he spoke to himself: "Yet I will keep the gold. His old mother with her weeping tale as to how she had borrowed the gold from the moneylender who would charge a hundred per cent for it! Huh! and why not? What reason is there to be a Qadi if there be no gold in it? Am I expected to suffer for the misdoings of these wanderers from the paths of accuracy?"

"Besides," he further argued, "the more afraid the mothers are of my desire to place their sons once more upon the slippery path leading to truth's approach, the more gold will they bring! Ha! Ha! more gold." Rubbing his hands he continued: "I am indeed a man to be reckoned with! Thus will my fame spread, and my gold chest be more and more augmented." He stroked his beard.

Advancing to the window and taking the mirror, he looked closely at the russet beard from every angle. It had been dyed to perfection.

Hitherto in the Qadi's court this great white beard had been to a prisoner the white flag of his personal surrender and defeat.

So far as the court was concerned the owner of the beard might, without interference, have allowed the shrivelled fingers of Time to stray permanently through it.

But there was the private life of the Qadi to be considered.

That day it had been considerably overset by the news one of his spies had brought of the ravishing beauty of Kulsum, the daughter of one Sekander Khan, the carpet merchant.

She, even with half that elegance and grace would still be worth having! At the very thought of the possession of her charms the Qadi felt no more than twenty again.

"The matter of the forty years' disparity in our ages will be overcome by the thought of becoming the wife of the Qadi," and here Jalal struck his breast, and straightened his back at the exciting thought of his importance.

"Never shall I be younger, and no time is as the present. At once will I hie me to the carpet merchant. The girl is mine even before the asking."

Sekander was honoured by the personal visit of the renowned Qadi, but slightly uneasy as to the reason for the distinction.

The two were now ensconced in the little business room behind the shop, and the carpet merchant watched the guest anxiously as he drew smoke from the newly charged hubble-bubble. Watched him as a man does another who holds his life in the cavity of a hand. The merchant was no mind-reader, and had to wait for the other to speak first.

After the usual side-tracking around a dozen different subjects, the Qadi approached the one which accounted for his presence, straight as an arrow from the bow.

"You have a daughter, Sekander Khan?"

"Three, Qadi Sahib."

"Yes, but only one unmarried?"

"As you say, Qadi Sahib."

"It is my desire to take her to wife."

The announcement caused the cleverly veiled reluctance to look like surprise on the face of the carpet merchant.

But this only increased both the Qadi's pleasure and his chances, for at precisely the same moment both men remembered there was that in the past life of Sekander Khan which could place him yet in the power of the relentless court of the Qadi; and this judge of the Sultan could pronounce irrevocable sentences.

For a few brief agonizing seconds the merchant realized his danger; then, dashing a shaking hand across his eyes, he turned to meet the half-mocking smile on the face of the Qadi.

And something whispered to him that the other recollected, knew that he was even then chewing the cud of bitter memories, so sweet in the mouth of the Qadi.

"Your consent and blessing, Sekander Khan?"

The words made Sekander recoil as from a snake.

"Only yesterday, Qadi sahib, was I engaged with the coppersmith on the subject of Kulsum's betrothal to his son."

"Ah! I am not too late then. It is well. Much gold have I and many jewels to give to the fair Kulsum!"

Sekander Khan shivered as from a sudden draught. Well he knew whence the gold came.

Was it not blood-money squeezed from distracted mothers whose sons were even now rotting in the city prisons? Gold for which these deranged women would have to toil all their lives; toil in vain . . .

Were the jewels not the cherished belongings which wives had stripped from their persons in a final heart-wrung appeal for a less harsh sentence on their husbands, as they grovelled on the ground in front of the merciless Qadi?

All this Sekander Khan knew, and more, and yet to stand up for his principles with judgement hanging over his very head . . .

The Qadi broke his silence.

"Your reluctance can be well understood, Sekander, as Kulsum is the only daughter left to you," glossily pleasant went on the voice of the Qadi.

"Nay, it is not reluctance, Qadi Sahib."

"Then it is your consent?"

"Y-yes!"

"Ah! I knew it, you are not the one to marry your daughter to

159

a penniless man."

Sekander Khan, to hide his anxiety, was loud in the praises of his daughter's wit, beauty, and accomplishments, all of which one would not have thought the Qadi was hearing for the second time.

The marriage was arranged for the next Friday, and the Qadi was easy in his mind, as he took leave of his future father-in-law.

The night before the wedding Kulsum and Fazil Hayat, the son of the coppersmith, bade farewell to each other.

"You know, Fazil, my beloved, I go as a sacrifice to the hated Qadi. Never willingly would I be wife to him. I have told you how he would have my father imprisoned and tortured. We all know and dread the power of the Qadi."

Fazil held her while she wept. He was overcome and almost beyond speech. All he was conscious of was that they would part for ever, and that the future held nothing for him.

"My heart is as pulp, and my blood as water in my veins," she whispered.

"Always shall I remember you, Kulsum; always will the memory be torture." He murmured to her hair as he enfolded her.

"Farewell, dearest Fazil, my father is calling."

"Farewell! My Beloved, this parting tears my heart from my body. Allah be with you!"

The next day Kulsum went to her new husband's home. To say she went willingly was contradicted by her swollen eyes, but if the Qadi noticed any indifference on the part of his lovely young bride, the very considerable amount of jewellery left by her two predecessors would, he surmised, soon pacify her. The days passed and the Qadi, seeing no visible signs of regret on the face of Kulsum, took this to be a good omen, for the Qadi knew women, or flattered himself he did; as many a man before had, since has, and in future will, persuade himself of the same fallacy.

Just what a good judge of women as well as of men he was, the Qadi was completely assured, when his wife anxiously persuaded him to engage a scribe, who would write up his court cases, and relieve him of much heavy work.

As luck would have it, a few days later a man visited the Qadi and pleaded to be given some work. It appeared that this Ghulam Hussain was well able to undertake what was required of him, and was engaged at once to begin.

His youth, however, began gradually to annoy the Qadi, and make him feel as old as his beard before it was hennaed.

A few weeks later, Qadi Jalal thought he noticed looks being exchanged between the scribe and Kulsum.

Without saying anything to either of them, he pretended to absent himself, while he was really secreted where he had an uninterrupted view of the two.

His fears were soon justified, and, angered beyond endurance he swept out of the house, anxious to get away from the deceitful lovers.

Just as he reached the gate of the courtyard, one of his spies approached it.

The news he brought was as oil to the flames of his rage.

He learned that the scribe, Ghulam Hussain, was none other than the chosen one of Kulsum, the son of the coppersmith with a changed name.

A plot leaped into his head.

Was not he, the Qadi, a master-plotter? Hush!

He would not crush the life out of this viper with its smooth-tongued hypocrisy in his garden of delight as he longed to do.

Rather would he take time and ruminate over the matter.

He might make a plan whereby the premature death of the designing double-tongued scribe might be placed in other hands than his own.

Next day a note thrown surreptitiously into the Qadi's room read:

"Beware! Qadi, oppressor of the poor! Make your peace with Allah. This night will be your last."

For some minutes the Qadi combed his beard thoughtfully with his fingers. Then he laughed; and laughed again.

Herein might lie the key to open the door of difficulties. Herein could be the answer to the prayer of the faithful. A plot had matured.

By this time the same spy returned breathless from the bazaar, where he had heard whisperings of the plot to kill the Qadi.

161

But Qadi Jalal only smiled broader and broader; an unusual procedure for a man threatened with sure, sudden, and violent death within the next few hours.

That night when the usual hour for coffee came, accompanied by the scribe, he proceeded as was his wont to the café. They occupied a table at the rear of the dimly-lit room in a furtive manner.

Both men were uneasy. Only the scribe showed it, for he felt, although it might only be his imagination, the eyes of his master upon him. And who knew but that the Qadi could read what he tried to hide, that even then, at that very minute, Kulsum, who rightly belonged to him, Fazil, was awaiting him in the shade of the great spreading pipul tree.

How distressed would she be at his absence, for that morning the Qadi had given him work which would occupy his time until midnight, and excuse him from the visit to the café. There had been no way of letting her know. His master was ordering more tea, which meant at least the long-drawn-out drinking of three more cups.

"Of a surety Sheitan himself seemed to have lent his aid to the Qadi this night," mumbled the scribe into his beard.

Here, however, his difficulties seemed to have but started, for the Qadi was speaking.

"I find I have forgotten an important paper, which ought to be delivered to a friend tonight, so that I shall be obliged to return home for it."

"Rather allow me to go," said the scribe, seeing a way out of the difficulty of meeting Kulsum.

"Nay, you remain here. I shall return in half-an-hour, but if by that time I am not here, come to my house."

Once outside, the Qadi chortled deeply and gratifyingly into his hennaed beard.

"We shall see, without a doubt we shall see!" he hummed. "To think that this dog, the son of a dog, thinks he can repulse me, the Qadi!"

He cleared his throat and spat fiercely.

Inside the café the time dragged for the uneasy scribe. Would Kulsum be discovered waiting for him, and the Qadi return but to strangle him? Apprehensively, he put his fingers to his throat and kept them there, while from time to time he glanced furtively at the door at the back of the café through which his master had disappeared.

When the half-hour at last had passed and no Qadi returned, Fazil Hayat rose from the table, and saw what had escaped his eyes before, the Qadi's cloak, easy to recognize as it was unlike any other, hanging on the peg beside him.

"Typical of the Qadi is this cloak," mused the scribe. "Always has this richly embroidered garment of distinctive cut and pattern been the object of my desire. The respect which it commands and receives wherever it appears! To think that he who has robbed me of my dear love, he who possesses the power of life and death over all of us, should be the possessor of a garment the very appearance of which reduces all to obeisance such as only a Holy Man should expect. Pah!"

One more look round the room and it was the work of a second to slip the cloak round his shoulders; the Qadi's chain of office round his neck.

Outside the front of the café, the scribe halted for a few seconds, making up his mind as to the direction he would take.

Presently he felt, rather than saw, a figure draw alongside him. As he turned quickly his heart almost missed a beat, for there at his side was—Kulsum! Kulsum in another distinctive cloak of the Qadi!

"On seeing my husband return alone I had to come here to see whether anything had happened to you, but to come undisguised was not possible. Like this I am safe," she said. "I greatly feared my husband had discovered our meetings, and I am sure he knows."

She did not tell him that her arms were covered with bruises, because she had refused the day before, to remain in the harem.

"How did you dare to come, my Kulsum?"

"Dare! There is nothing one would not dare for love. Besides so unhappy am I that death itself would be a good friend to me. How my heart aches for the old days at home!"

The two lovers walked on whispering together, little dreaming what Fate was planning for them at that very moment.

Meanwhile, two muffled figures were stealthily following the pair.

"Which is the Qadi?" asked one.

"Both wear the cloaks of the Qadi, suppose neither is he?"

"We must kill the Qadi, to earn the promised gold."

"Would not I kill two Qadis for half the sum?"

"No dead Qadi, no bright gold. Let us make sure of both."

"Even so, but suppose, brother, we kill two and neither is the Qadi, then our necks are likely to be longer than our purses!"

"What then to do?"

"Let us repair to the house of the Qadi, and there await his homecoming, thus placing ourselves where the gold will be more of a certainty."

The hired assassins hid themselves where they could observe all without being seen.

The Qadi meanwhile, maddened by the hate he bore the scribe who had robbed him of the love of Kulsum, determined to let her know he was aware of what she and her lover here pleased to think their own secret.

He would go to her apartments, and face her with the truth, bolstered by hope that by now the writers of the anonymous threats on his life would undoubtedly have carried out their threat.

Accordingly he crossed the courtyard to the harem apartments and knocked. It was apparently locked inside, and this further maddened the enraged man.

"Open the door, woman," he yelled. "It is thy husband! the Qadi, not thy lover! Thy lover is *dead*! *Dead in the cloak of the Qadi*!"

Still there was no response from within.

The coarse laugh died in his throat as he turned to be confronted by two muffled figures.

They needed no further proof of the identity of their victim.

"We come from the sons of Akbar Aziz, to avenge the cruel death of their father, wrongfully accused and tortured to death by your orders."

The Qadi's beard parted, but no word came. The assassins were there to see that none ever would pass those lips again.

Truly, as the Persians say: "A jackal in a lion's skin is still a jackal."

* * *

"My name is Hari Ram, or, rather, that is the name given me

by my parents, worthy people of Kashmir settled in Delhi nowadays," said one of the Afghan's guests, "but, since I became a Moslem I am known as *Taslim*—Reconciled—and I have thought a great deal about the narratives which we in the East hear and tell and hear again.

"I now present you a story which passes among us for a tragedy and which many of my people, as even do those of the West, regard as something to provoke a tear.

"Listen well, and think deeply, so that perhaps, at some time, its import may break through your desire only to be entertained."

The story was—The Pearl of Kashmir.

THE PEARL OF KASHMIR

Moti, they called her, which, in the vernacular, means Pearl. Her real name was Lotus Blossom because, notwithstanding the fact that she was a girl and therefore of small moment, she was able to attract a certain amount of attention at her birth. She was born on the banks of the Dal Lake in fair Kashmir. The lotus lilies were out when she was ushered precipitately into this world—the Kashmir women regard childbirth with an amazing nonchalance—and it was observed, as she lay kicking her tiny heels in the sun, that she had an ivory skin. It was tinged with a delicate shade of pink and the texture reminded those who saw it of the soft velvety peaches which the hillmen bring down from their mountain fastnesses. She resembled the lilies floating serenely upon the lake. On the spot she was named Lotus Blossom.

She grew to maidenhood, and the pinkness faded. The velvet texture and the ivory remained. Her face was rounded, and her figure petite. The men, when they discussed her in the bazaars of Srinigar, or upon the floating homes on the fast-flowing Jhelum, spoke of her as Moti, the Pearl.

Her father was a wood-carver. He cut and chiselled at the hard, mountain walnut in a tiny room near the Third Bridge. He was a poor man. He provided his family with rice, with condiments and, very occasionally, with goat.

Moti disliked goat. There was a harsh tang to its flavour and she was learning to be fastidious. She demanded mutton.

Gopal Chand, her father, lifted his hands in horror. When he had recovered from his surprise, he picked up a shoe, and the wails of the erring Moti filled the bazaar.

Moti disappeared. She was then twelve, and therefore a girl ripe for marriage. Gopal Chand regarded the matter philosophically. Since she had gone there would be no necessity to visit the moneylender in order to raise a dowry when the time came.

Now and again, travellers from Kashmir to the plains of the Indus brought news of Moti. When she was fourteen it was rumoured that she was queening it in the bazaars of Rawalpindi. A year later, it was confidently rumoured that she was in the care of a rich Sikh at Amritsar. These were the days of wars and of unceasing conflict, and reliable information was difficult to obtain.

Still later, it was said that Moti had migrated to Delhi, doubtless attracted by the splendours of the Moghul court.

There it was that she encountered her first opposition. As a courtesan she had to learn finesse and refinement. The courtly circles demanded more than an ivory complexion and an impeccable figure.

Moti found herself one of a queue of Oriental enchantresses, all anxious to catch the royal eye and the favours which this brought in its train.

Moti had visions of rich, silken raiment from the weavers of Tehran, of pearls brought from the mystical shores of Japan, of gold anklets and nose ornaments fashioned by the craftsmen of Delhi from the mines of the far-off State of Mysore.

The way was hard, and it promised to be long. There were many in the regal entourage who looked kindly upon her and promised, with fair words, to bring her into the path of the Emperor, but Moti had learnt to be cautious. She preferred to remain aloof. She was learning finesse. Rawalpindi, Amritsar, and other episodes in her life could be submerged in the past. There, in Delhi, within the radiance of the court, it was necessary to be circumspect. Otherwise—a brief fling, and one descended to the bazaars.

Moti had other plans. She decided to lay seige to the army.

On moonlight nights, when light and shadows were sharply defined and the ivory of her skin played entrancingly with the moonbeams, she would occasionally be seen near the Pearl Mosque, just within the outer walls of the citadel. There it was that the haughty officers of the Emperor's Guard were wont to promenade.

Twice was she accidentally discovered in this romantic setting.

Subadar Samandar Khan, a stern and soldierly figure, as befitted the captain of the Guard, was the first of her victims.

167

He saw a sylph-like figure and challenged. He advanced, hand upon the hilt of his *talwar,* and he discovered two large eyes, glistening like immense opals, gazing up at him in fright. As he advanced, the figure shrank back from the walls of the Mosque. It stood out in sharp relief. The sari, clutched round the form with two tremulous hands, accentuated and made obvious to the masculine eye the perfection of the girl's figure.

Subadar Samandar Khan gazed hard. He hesitated. He gazed again. He was enmeshed.

The Subadar was no gallant. He was content to feast his eyes upon this radiating star. He regarded Moti as some fragile piece of priceless china. Every whim, but half expressed, was a command. He was enslaved.

Jamadar Akram Khan, too, discovered her in her moonlight setting. He was of vastly different calibre. He was a devil-may-care swashbuckler, and he had the reputation of being a great lover.

Moti was well able to deal with the type—her education had been thorough since the paternal slipper had fallen so agonizingly.

She tantalized the man. She played with him—and she laughed at him. Once, in one of his more passionate moments, she drew a small dagger from the folds of her sari. She pricked him gently on the breast. He fell back with an oath, eyes ablaze with anger.

Both men were sure—and yet, not so sure. Both lived through many nights of excruciating mental torture.

Both knew of the other's passion. The situation was fraught with difficulties which could sap regimental discipline.

There was trouble also, within the bodyguard.

The Sikhs were pressing forward through the Punjab, threatening the existence of the Moghul court. There were those of the bodyguard who said that Delhi must fall as it did when the emperor Nadir Shah ransacked the treasuries but a few years before.

The Jamadar was one of these and he counselled diplomacy. "If Delhi must fall," he said, "then it must—Kismet, Fate—and the Sikhs, it is said, make good masters."

The pressure from the Punjab grew more insistent. It was said that the Sikhs were preparing to advance beyond Lahore.

The mutterings within the bodyguard came to a head. A section, under the Jamadar, broke away and endeavoured to make itself master of the magazine by the Delhi Gate, later to be blown up during the days of the 1857 Rising.

The trouble spread to the bazaars. Delhi was in turmoil.

The rebels held that part of the city surrounding the magazine. They were given twenty-four hours in which to evacuate their position, failing which, the loyal troops under Subadar Samandar Khan, would attack and destroy them to a man.

Moti had to make a decision. She had either to declare herself for the Subadar or incline towards the Jamadar and the revolutionaries.

She chose the Jamadar. That night she took up her quarters within the magazine.

Next morning at dawn, there was the attack—and the orders from the court were that there was to be no quarter.

Delhi lived through a bloody day, but, at night-fall, the mutineers, their ranks sadly depleted, still held possession.

There were pourparlers and an intimation was sent to the mutineers.

They had an hour to vacate the magazine. Thereafter, declared the Subadar, he would train the palace guns upon the magazine and send it sky-high together with all those within it.

To the Jamadar the Subadar sent a special, secret, message. He implored him to send Moti away from the danger zone while there was yet time.

The answer came back. A small round object wrapped in a silk handkerchief. It was a ripe lime which, in the East, has the same significance which some Westerners attach to a lemon.

The hour of grace went by and the mutineers remained. Still the Subadar hesitated.

Word came from the palace to press home the attack.

Disobeying orders, the Subadar withheld the fire of his cannon and personally led another onslaught. The fighting was fierce and the dusty roads around the magazine became a quagmire of blood. Weight told, however, as it eventually must in such matters, and by midnight the Subadar, clutching his dripping *talwar*, burst into the magazine.

"No quarter" was the cry and Samandar Khan gazed

anxiously around for Moti. The interior of the magazine was a shambles, but nowhere could he discern any sign of that brightly coloured sari.

Jamadar Akram Khan lay groaning in a corner. A great slashing blow had cut through his shoulder blade.

Samandar Khan strode toward him, kicking aside the bodies.

"This is sorry work, Jamadar," he said, as he gazed down at the bleeding man. "Where is Moti?"

The grey lips of the man upon the ground pursed into a semblance of a smile.

"Moti is in a house a hundred yards away," he answered. "She is within call. I managed to get her out during our armistice, but she declared that she would remain near."

"She loves you as much as that?"

The Jamadar opened the palm of his left hand. It was the only gesture of which he was capable, but it was expressive.

The man on the ground looked up.

"I heard the cry, 'No quarter'," he said, haltingly. "Why do you hesitate?"

The Subadar started.

"Come, why do you wait?"

Samandar Khan raised his glittering *talwar* and then paused. He saw the mocking eyes of the prostrate man before him. He lowered his sword arm.

"Would you play with me like a dog?"

There was a jeering note in the Jamadar's query.

Samandar Khan spoke slowly, and with deliberation.

"You are a dog," he said, "and worthy of the fate of a dog. But, because of a woman, I will forget my duty. I will leave you here. If you can contrive to escape, perhaps Moti will be happy."

Samandar Khan stalked away. In his report of the fighting he made it clear that there had been no mercy shown. He was unprepared, however, for the persistence displayed by the Emperor. It was decreed that the body of Jamadar Akram Khan should be suspended from the walls of the fort in order that all might observe the fate of those who incurred the royal displeasure.

There was no body and the Subadar was confronted with a

problem. He solved it by confession. He craved an audience of the Emperor and told him of his fault.

The Emperor, furious and unnerved by recent events, declared that an example must be made.

There must be a body, he said, and as Samandar Khan had created the deficiency he must likewise make it good.

The Emperor smiled at the profundity of his wit.

"Take him away," he roared. "At dawn, shoot him, and place his body at the spot where that of Akram Khan should now be providing meat for the vultures."

Samandar Khan was led away. He consoled himself, as best he could, with thoughts of Moti and the great happiness which would be hers because of the sacrifice which he was making.

Just before dawn they came to fetch him.

As he prepared for his journey to the foot walls, the red sandstone of which would shortly take on a splash of more sombre hue, he asked of Akram Khan.

"Did he get away?" he queried of his jailers.

"No," responded the officer in charge, sympathetically, "It would have been better if you had used your sword. He was found at a house one hundred yards from the magazine."

"He died of that sword thrust?"

"No. There was a dagger in his heart."

Beads of perspiration came to Samandar Khan's forehead.

"Have you any news of Moti, the woman?" he asked.

The officer smiled.

"Yes," he said. "The house where Akram Khan was found belongs to the premier, the Dewan. It is said in the bazaars that the Dewan has a new mistress. Rumour says that she is a Kashmiri and that she is of ivory skin."

Samandar Khan bowed his head.

"We will proceed," he said with dignity. "You have a duty to perform."

* * *

There was one man left, in our Mecca nightly gathering, who had given us no tale, but who had always listened to the others with the very greatest attention. Stooped and scholarly, with a pair of metal-rimmed spectacles, he looked every inch the private secretary whom one might find in the palace of a prince. I realised how good my guess was when he at last began his tale, that of The Haunted Carpet.

THE HAUNTED CARPET

"I had no real reason to dislike the Prince of Jutpore whose territory I entered as a guest," he said, "but that I did dislike him, detested him, had been obvious to me from the moment he had engaged me as his secretary. I loathed the atmosphere of his gloomy palace on the outskirts of the ancient little city, I hated the dreadful room in which I had to work. But I was not the master of my own fortunes and therefore could not but endure the surroundings I execrated.

Not only was the Prince haughty and monosyllabic, mysterious and, to my mind, ill-balanced, but he was certainly the most ill-favoured human being I had ever set eyes on. His pale unhealthy face had all the cold horror of a death mask in plaster, and the lustreless eyes, which could scarcely be said to light it, resembled those of a dead man. The great room in which he laboured so ceaselessly at his work of reading and transcribing was stifling, dark and neglected, for he would permit no one to lay an orderly hand upon its dire confusion. Almost directly behind his chair stood an immense piece of furniture of a type and workmanship altogether unfamiliar to me. It was made of some exceptionally hard wood, and every square inch of its surface was richly carved with grotesque symbols, regarding the purport of which I could not even hazard a guess. Serpents writhed and twined upon its sides, and in the centre of each of its two doors, leering faces, crowned with feathers, were surrounded by an intricate wealth of ornamental detail, which had for me not the faintest significance. A lamp of bizarre appearance and extraordinary workmanship hung from the roof, and even the chair in which the Prince sat was of a weird and antique shape.

But, most striking of all the curious things that this repellent yet fascinating room contained, was the wonderful carpet which occupied a portion of the spacious stone-flagged floor, and which lay in all its arresting display of colour and pattern between my employer's desk and the door. As no furniture was placed on it, not even a chair or settee, it was easy to get a full view of it in all its beauty or hideousness—for to this day I cannot make up my mind regarding the essential quality through which it appealed to me; at times attracting, at others repulsing me by virtue of the strange properties which seemed to reside in its unusual colours and eccentric design. Of what material it was made I could not at first satisfy myself, but I found later that it had been woven from the fibre of the jute plant, and the details of its workmanship left no doubt in my mind that it had been fashioned by native weavers.

The ground of this peculiar carpet was a shade of golden-yellow or honey colour, with which a mysterious and perplexing design had been interwoven. Fringing the border was a series of discs in blue and red which seemed to me to represent eyes—not human eyes, but round bird-like orbs, half closed, yet unwinking, holding both the solemn stare of the owl and the brooding menace of the vulture. Within this border, ranks of great red spiders with human faces sprawled to meet a row of undulant serpents and spotted toads. The centre was occupied by a grim yellow skull, from whose sockets a pair of eyes just like those fringing the edges of the carpet looked out balefully. The effect of the whole was that of a craftsmanship barbarous, yet artistic, and I did not know which to admire more—the almost unique skill shown in the wonderfully involved design, or the warm shades of the brilliant and realistic dyes with which it had been coloured. But this notwithstanding, the aversion I felt at times to this singular piece of workmanship was so intense that I could scarcely bring myself to remain in the same room with it. At other times I could scarcely tear myself away from the contemplation of its striking pattern and gorgeous hues.

By degrees I came to the conclusion that the carpet was a thing accursed. Its extraordinary symbols haunted me. I dreaded it, while it fascinated me. The Prince noticed the attention I paid to it, and once said unsmilingly:

"If you will take my advice Mr. Secretary," for this was always the way in which he addressed me, "you will not look upon that carpet too curiously. It—well, it has a history."

And then something happened which aroused my slumbering fears to active terror. One night, about eleven o'clock, I suddenly recalled that I had left some unfinished work upon my desk. I hastened to the great room to lock it away. Entering abruptly I found a sight which I still cannot think of without horror.

The Prince stood in the centre of the room. Where the lamp glowed brightly, an oasis of light in a desert of gloomy shadow, he stood. His face wore a fixed and terrible expression. To my amazement I saw that his cheeks were daubed with red and black paint, he was dressed in a flowing robe of crimson—and his arms were red to the elbows as if with blood. The doors of the great armoury behind him, I do not know how to describe it otherwise, stood open wide, and I had a glimpse of barbaric implements, gilded, carved, grotesquely appalling in their smiling and symbolic hideousness.

Coming suddenly upon such a sight, was it surprising that I exclaimed loudly—cried out in horror? As I did so, his weird, languorous eyes turned quickly in my direction, and lit up with cruel yellow fires, like those of a savage beast.

"How dare you come here?" he thundered. "Go—at once—instantly."

I went—quickly. What in heaven's name had I witnessed? I could not even guess. I spent a night of anxious and troubled surmise. When I entered his room next morning he beckoned me to his desk.

"Mr. Secretary," he said in his ordinary level tones, "I would prefer it if you did not enter this room after ten o'clock at night. I frequently engage in experiments, the delicate nature of which scarcely admits of sudden intrusion. Do I make myself plain?"

I assured him that I perfectly understood his dislike of interruption.

I did my best to put what I had seen out of my mind, but with little success. Indeed, I grew almost morbidly interested in the personality of my strange employer. The prince might be insane, his midnight performance might be dictated by a mind diseased. But how was I to account for the extraordinary situation, the weird costume in which I had surprised him on that night—how explain the painted face, the blood-red robe? Surely the whole thing was too outrageous to exist outside of a madhouse.

Strive as I might, I found it impossible to banish the memory of what I had glimpsed that midnight. The whole fantastic circumstances had burned themselves into my brain. They were with me at my rising and my lying down. And the more I brooded upon them, the more I became conscious that meditation upon the strange nature of my surroundings was bringing me into touch with some force, some power, subtle and malignant. As I sat at my work, I recalled my first entrance into this room, the revulsion I had experienced. I cursed myself for a fool, rallied myself in that spirit of irony which is perhaps the surest indication of fear. But to no purpose. And then, one day, certainty took the place of surmise.

As I sat alone at the window of the Prince's room one late afternoon busied with my work, I became aware of a certain slackness, an interruption of the sober spirit of occupation. At the imperious call of some outer impulse, I raised my eyes from the papers with which I was engaged and looked behind me. The great room was full of the shadows of the hour before evening. At first, from where I sat, I could scarcely see the wall opposite me. But as my eyes grew accustomed to the gloomy interior, I could perceive no signs of human presence. I knew that the Prince was in the city. And yet I could have been certain that that which had made me glance so hurriedly over my shoulder was born of the natural instinct we experience when under observation. Urged by some kind of nervous energy, I rose and walked half-way to the door. But strain my eyes as I might in peering down the dark length of the place, I could see nothing; listen as I might, hear nothing.

I returned to my seat. In another moment I was as engrossed as ever in my work. For perhaps a quarter of an hour I scribbled on, looking neither right nor left. Then I became dimly conscious of a rustling like the movement of a light and nimble body. I swung round in my chair, every sense strung to its uttermost by instinctive panic. The rustling noise continued. Straining my eyes through the fast-gathering darkness, I saw the outline of something huge and yellow writhing in slow and sinuous agitation. *The carpet . . . was moving!*

Leaping from my seat, I seized a heavy stick which always lay beside the Prince's chair, and ran forward. The carpet lay absolutely motionless. A rat, I supposed, had got beneath it. I struck at it again and again, in the passion of resentment which comes of sudden shock.

I did my utmost to forget about the carpet, telling myself that I had been the victim of a mere hallucination. All the same I found it impossible to rid myself of the feeling that something uncanny lurked within its brilliant folds. This was by no means allayed by something which happened not many days later.

Selecting at random a book for evening reading, I chanced upon a bound manuscript volume in the Prince's library. It was evidently a personal diary written by a British official about a century before—in the John Company days—and in turning its yellow leaves I suddenly saw the following passages:—

"Indeed my Maria has a profound objection to the carpet, and insists, the dear creature, that it has a life of its own. Strange, is it not, that we discovered the syce (groom) quite dead, wrapt in its hideous folds? How grossly superstitious the people here are, to be sure. But that Maria should harbour such absurd conjectures. . . . When I put down my pen just now it was because of cries in the courtyard below. It seems that Fanny, our Yorkshire nurse, rushed screaming into the withdrawing room shrieking that the carpet had risen at her, and struck out at her with one of its corners, for all the world like a great serpent. I must rid myself of the pestilential thing. I shall sell it—or burn it, preferably the latter. The cook assures me it is the property of Kali, the goddess of human sacrifice."

A page or two further on I found this passage:

"Lord have mercy upon us! The accursed carpet. My unhappy child! What a catastrophe! I can write no more."

What the nature of the "catastrophe" had been, or who was the "unhappy child" referred to, I never discovered, for here the manuscript ended. I was in the act of replacing it in the bookcase, when a sinuous motion beneath my feet made me leap backward. That part of the carpet between my window and the desk was agitated violently as though by a gust of wind, and that although it was a calm and windless evening. Then, to my horror, it rose in the air: a full three feet and more.

How I managed to escape from that dreadful room I cannot say. I only know that I found myself on the other side of the window in the bright moonlight, trembling and utterly demoralized. Making my way out of the garden I walked for miles into the country like a man in a dream, before I found the courage to return to the house.

And as I did so, I remembered. It was the night of the full moon, the night of the immemorial sacrifice to the blood-drenched goddess Kali, the most fiendish and barbarous of all the deities of India. I was aware, of course, that her worship had been proscribed and absolutely forbidden by the English Raj, but I trembled with fear even to think of the abomination manifestly dedicated to her which lay on the floor of that detestable room. But the better part of my courage had returned, and as I entered the garden and saw a light burning in the Prince's apartment, I felt sufficiently emboldened to march right up to the window to see what he was doing.

As I peered through the glass I recoiled in horror. Once more with distorted countenance and blood-red hands the Prince stood in the middle of the room, making what seemed to me magical passes, the light of a fanatical frenzy in his eyes. The carpet, lay, as it seemed to me, like a dragon half asleep, its frightful half-closed eyes yet balefully awake.

"Kali!" shrieked the Prince, and I could hear him through the closed window, "Hear me, Kali! This very night shall I render to thee the heart's blood of the accursed man who sleeps above, and who is so in my power. Six lives hast thou had in as many years, and with this, the seventh, my task shall be complete, and I shall hence-forth be thy high priest. Kali! Kali! Hear me, Goddess of the Abyss!"

So it was for this that the Prince had engaged me as his secretary. A terrible feeling of revulsion surged over me. From fear I rose to the heights of an angry disgust. That this demon should have selected me as his victim appeared to me not only as a deep personal wrong, but as an infamy both to my own faith and to the essence of the Hindu religion which I respected and even admired for its beauty and spirituality. This degraded creature of a savage cult horrible to all true men, ruinous to India, must be made to suffer for his abominations. Yes, tonight, despite his rank, I would see to it that he was placed beyond the power to cause further outrage.

Suddenly, as I stood there trembling, I noticed that on which the Prince stood move slightly. Then there was a swift and voluminous uprising of something . . . something which surged and billowed round him in vast and enveloping folds, like great yellow waves flecked with a multicoloured foam. He stood for an instant in awful amazement. Then a look of such terror crossed his face as I have never seen in that of living man.

Even as he screamed, the carpet with its riot of dreadful symbols, wound itself about him, its sides shrouding his head, its corners writhing around his limbs like the tentacles of an octopus. The serpent and spider shapes with which it was covered seemed to move in an awful mimicry of life, while from every part of the whirling mass the dreadful half-closed eyes looked out, alight, as it seemed, with demon fire. Powerless to aid, and, as I believe, in the grip of some malignant and arresting force, I stood at the window while the yells of the suffocating wretch grew fainter and fainter. Through the folds of the woven mass which surrounded him, I could see the writhing of his limbs. His howls died away to a low moaning. At last, when the power of movement returned to me and I rushed forward, a dreadful stillness had replaced the anguished struggling of the moment before. The carpet lay flattened and creaseless upon the floor. And upon its bizarre background huddled the Prince, the secret priest of the goddess Kali, with purple and distorted face—dead.

* * *

"In cruder assemblies than that in which we now find ourselves," said the Secretary as he finished his tale, "people would think this recital something designed to freeze the blood, the class of tale which people in the West call accounts of hauntings or of horror. To us, of course, the message is that only by analogy can it be conveyed with true stress that there are forces in the mind and in inanimate objects, too, which perform tasks upon this earth in a manner only dimly understood by even the most intelligent of men.

"This, of course, must be the reason why, interpreted by shallow minds, accounts of unusual forces and of the workings of the mind still remain unplumbed for their real meaning, except among those who prefer to know than to be made excited."

For further information on this subject please write to:—

THE SOCIETY FOR SUFI STUDIES
P.O. BOX 43   LOS ALTOS
CALIFORNIA 94022   USA